PORTFOLIO
Published by the Penguin Group
Penguin Group (USA) Inc., 375 Hudson Street, New York, New York 10014, U.S.A. ● Penguin
Group (Canada), 90 Eglinton Avenue East, Suite 700, Toronto, Ontario, Canada M4P 2Y3
(a division of Pearson Penguin Canada Inc.) ● Penguin Books Ltd, 80 Strand, London WC2R
0RL, England ● Penguin Ireland, 25 St. Stephen's Green, Dublin 2, Ireland (a division of Pen-
guin Books Ltd) ● Penguin Books Australia Ltd, 250 Camberwell Road, Camberwell, Victoria
3124, Australia (a division of Pearson Australia Group Pty Ltd) ● Penguin Books India Pvt
Ltd, 11 Community Centre, Panchsheel Park, New Delhi – 110 017, India ● Penguin Group
(NZ), 67 Apollo Drive, Rosedale, North Shore 0632, New Zealand (a division of Pearson New
Zealand Ltd) ● Penguin Books (South Africa) (Pty) Ltd, 24 Sturdee Avenue, Rosebank,
Johannesburg 2196, South Africa

Penguin Books Ltd, Registered Offices:
80 Strand, London WC2R 0RL, England

First published in 2009 by Portfolio,
a member of Penguin Group (USA) Inc.

10 9 8 7 6 5 4 3 2 1

LIBRARY OF CONGRESS CATALOGING IN PUBLICATION DATA
Monica, Paul R. La.
Inside Rupert's brain / Paul R. La Monica.
p.   cm.
Includes bibliographical references and index.
978-1-59184-243-9
1. Murdoch, Rupert, 1931– 2. Mass media—Biography. 3. Mass media—Management.
4. Businesspeople—Biography. I. Title.
P92.5.M87M66 2009
302.23—dc22   2008028601

Printed in the United States of America
Set in Electra LT Regular and Rotis Serif with Myriad Pro
Designed by Daniel Lagin

INSIDE RUPERT'S BRAIN

INSIDE
RUPERT'S
BRAI

Paul R. La

A

LIB
Mo
Insi

Inclu
ISBN 9
1. Murd
4. Busin
P92.5.M
070.5092
[B]

Printed in t
Set in Vende
Designed by

To Beth. For everything.

CONTENTS

Preface   ix

Introduction   1

1. **Start Spreading the News**   15

2. **Crazy Like a Fox**   41

3. **Hooked on Cable**   68

4. **The Sky's the Limit**   93

5. **Wheeling and Dealing**   112

6. **Rupert 2.0**   145

7. **The Battle for Dow Jones**   168

8. **All in the Family**   202

Epilogue   226

Acknowledgments   239

Notes   241

Index   257

PREFACE

News Corp. chairman and CEO Rupert Murdoch is the man that many in the media love to hate. Murdoch is often demonized by journalists who work for competitors because of his political views and willingness to dictate news coverage when he sees fit. While Murdoch is far from being a saint, he has been often unfairly criticized by those who fail to understand that at the end of the day, the media business is still a business and that Murdoch likes to make money. In *Inside Rupert's Brain,* Paul R. La Monica takes a more sober and less emotional look at the controversial Murdoch's successes and failures. For better or for worse, Murdoch has transformed the news industry, Hollywood, and the rest of the media world. And very often, competitors who have criticized him have eventually gone on to imitate him, a fact that thrills Murdoch, the original media maverick. Still, Murdoch is a career newspaperman and the one thing that he has craved has been journalistic respect, something he has never been able to achieve by owning tabloids and a cable news channel that is largely viewed as having a right-wing bias. And with the media business in a period of flux, there are concerns that his \$5 billion gamble on Dow Jones may have been an overpriced mistake that had more to do about ego and less about profit.

INTRODUCTION

"**W**e're cooling on the idea of buying Dow Jones. The *Wall Street Journal* is obviously a wonderful brand. But I don't think we'd ever get it or they'd ever sell it."[1]

That's what News Corp. chairman and CEO Rupert Murdoch said to an audience of media executives at a conference sponsored by McGraw-Hill in New York, about the possibility of his media conglomerate buying the venerable publisher of the *Journal*. The date was February 8, 2007.

A little less than three months later, Murdoch's News Corp. launched its bold $5 billion, unsolicited takeover bid for Dow Jones. The offer valued Dow Jones, which had been struggling as more and more advertisers and readers were fleeing print for the Web, at a staggering 65 percent premium over its closing price the day before the bid was announced.

News Corp. announced its bid on May 1, 2007, and while it

would ultimately take Murdoch three months to convince the Bancroft family that controlled Dow Jones to agree to a sale, there were few doubts that he would eventually succeed. After all, while some media experts scratched their heads about why Murdoch would offer such an exorbitant sum for Dow Jones, many other media watchers knew that the bid was a perfect gambit.

Murdoch offered as much as he did in order to ensure that he would have no competition. And, as it turned out, that was precisely the case.

Offering $5 billion for Dow Jones wound up being too much to ask for investors such as Ron Burkle, a billionaire who made his money through supermarket properties, as well as Brian Tierney, the owner of the *Philadelphia Inquirer* and *Philadelphia Daily News*. The $5 billion price tag even scared off cash-rich publicly traded companies such as General Electric, Pearson and Microsoft.

The takeover bid from Murdoch, coming so soon after he publicly said that an offer was not likely, is a perfect example of Murdoch's maverick nature. Murdoch transformed News Corp. from a mere regional newspaper publisher to a global media giant with a leading presence in television, movies and now the Internet.

"Look at Murdoch and his history. News Corp. has gone from being just an Australian newspaper company and evolved that into a U.S. media and global satellite company. If anyone has the DNA to adapt and change, it's Murdoch," said Alan

Gould, an analyst who covers News Corp. for Wall Street investment bank Natixis Bleichroeder.[2]

But has Murdoch, with the purchase of Dow Jones, done a deal that will come back to haunt him? It's easy to understand why critics would say that buying a slow-growth newspaper publisher is a mistake. After all, with newspaper ad revenues plunging as readers abandon traditional print publications for blogs and other online news sources, many are proclaiming that the print industry is dying.

Some suggest Murdoch may also grow tired of Dow Jones if it does not wind up generating the type of strong growth that he will clearly demand from it. After all, a hallmark of the Murdoch strategy is his almost ceaseless deal making. And Murdoch has often quickly fallen out of love with assets he's acquired. During his tenure running News Corp., he's owned and sold brand-name publications such as *TV Guide*, *New York* magazine and the *Village Voice*, for example.

More recently, News Corp. bought the L.A. Dodgers baseball team in 1998 and sold it in 2004. The company also bought a stake in U.S. satellite television business in DirecTV in 2003, only to turn around in 2006 and announce that it was selling the stake to Liberty Media, the conglomerate owned by John Malone, a media rival and occasional thorn in Murdoch's side.

Some would argue that Murdoch has been savvy, buying and unloading assets at the right time, milking them for maximum profit. But others might argue that Murdoch's constant wheeling and dealing is an example of someone who is too willing to make aggressive bets on certain businesses regardless of whether they fit in his current portfolio. It hints at impulsiveness on his part as well.

To be sure, Murdoch has made his share of curious business decisions—strategic moves that have not always panned out the way that he, or News Corp. shareholders, would have hoped.

But another trademark of Murdoch's career is his willingness, more so than most other media executives, to take bold chances. His decisions have been scrutinized and often criticized by analysts, investors and insiders of the famously skeptical media industry.

However, Murdoch, more often than not, has had the last laugh.

"Investors have initially disagreed with the vast majority of News Corp.'s/Mr. Murdoch's acquisitions/investments historically," wrote Richard Greenfield, an analyst with Wall Street research firm Pali Research, in a report shortly after News Corp. announced its intention to buy Dow Jones. "Yet, the overwhelming majority of these deals/investments have created substantial value for News Corp. shareholders."

For example, when News Corp.'s Fox broadcast network debuted in 1986, few thought that a fourth prime-time network would be able to survive in a world that had been dominated for decades by ABC, CBS and NBC.

Yet Fox not only survived but thrived and has been responsible for some of the biggest pop culture media phenomena of the past two decades, including the show's long-running animated hit *The Simpsons*, teen soap opera *Beverly Hills 90210* and singing contest *American Idol*.

The latter show has been such a ratings juggernaut since it debuted in 2002 that executives at the other networks openly talk about the futility of programming against it and, with an almost reverential sense of awe, refer to *Idol* as the Death Star of prime-time television.

Murdoch also defied the odds when he took on Ted Turner in the cable news race. When News Corp. launched Fox News Channel in 1996, few believed that there would be enough of an audience to justify the existence of a second twenty-four-hour all-news network.

But yet again Murdoch's bold move paid off. Fox News, which boldly proclaims that the network simply has its news personalities report and lets viewers decide, now routinely beats archrival CNN in the ratings. Fox News is widely criticized by some media experts and Democratic politicians as simply being a mouthpiece for the Republican Party. But the network clearly tapped into a desire for more conservative viewpoints on television news, similar to the way many right-wing talk shows have thrived on radio.

Murdoch also has taken dramatic steps to make sure that News Corp. would not be left behind in the digital media race, most notably by purchasing MySpace. News Corp. decided to acquire Intermix Media, the parent company of the popular social networking site, for $580 million in July 2005. At the time, some analysts worried that Murdoch was paying too much for the still-unproven company.

MySpace, after all, was only founded in 2003 and there was much debate about whether social networking sites like MySpace would ever be able to generate the types of advertising revenue that would be needed to justify the amount of money News Corp. was paying for it.

Others feared that News Corp. would tinker with what made MySpace popular with teens and young adults looking to connect with each other as well as with singers and bands who used the site to promote their music. The thought was that users would flee MySpace in droves for other social networking sites in order to protest the fact that their "Place for Friends" was no longer a plucky upstart but was instead now a cog in the massive media conglomerate that also included the likes of Bill O'Reilly and the *New York Post* as corporate cousins.

But teens haven't rebelled against MySpace. In fact, the site became even more successful under Murdoch's ownership. As of January 2008, MySpace had nearly 300 million registered accounts and it was averaging 68.6 million unique visitors a month and 43.3 *billion* page views. That's up substantially from the 34 million registered users worldwide that MySpace had when News Corp. officially took it over in November 2005. And at that time, the site was only averaging 12.5 million unique visitors a month in the United States and 26.7 billion page views according to Web traffic research firm comScore.

"You were all laughing at me for buying MySpace," Murdoch told investors during a Goldman Sachs media conference in September 2007. "What's that worth today? It's worth more than twenty times what we paid for it."[3]

At the time of that remark, it seemed like this was just another example of Murdoch puffing his chest in order to prove that once again he had proved the skeptics wrong. However, several analysts were dubious of Murdoch's claim that MySpace's value could have increased from $580 million to $11.6 billion in just two years.

Yet only a month later, Murdoch's "guesstimate" about MySpace's value looked a lot more prescient. Microsoft bought a small stake in MySpace's top rival Facebook at a price that valued Facebook at a whopping $15 billion. And as Murdoch was fond of pointing out to anyone who'd listen, Facebook had fewer users and averaged a lower amount of monthly page views than MySpace.

So Dow Jones could turn out to be another success like MySpace, an asset that he could throw considerable marketing power behind to boost its sale and profit potential. And even if the Dow Jones purchase never winds up being a financial powerhouse for News Corp., owning the *Wall Street Journal* may give Murdoch something that can't be found on a profit-and-loss statement. It's something that many say he's been craving for decades: journalistic credibility and integrity.

Murdoch's tabloids, such as the *New York Post* and Britain's *Sun* and the weekly *News of the World*, aren't exactly known for hard-hitting, serious news. The *Journal*, on the other hand, is widely acknowledged as one of the best publications on the planet and certainly one of the most respected sources for business news.

To that end, some suggest that the acquisition of Dow Jones is more about ego than dollars and cents.

"This deal has been in his blood for twenty years. This is a deal of passion, not of spreadsheets," said Steven Rattner, managing principal with Quadrangle Group, a private equity firm, at a media conference in New York in October 2007.[4]

Rattner previously was an investment banker with Morgan Stanley during the 1980s and advised Murdoch when News Corp. bought a stake in Pearson, the British media conglomerate that owns the *Financial Times* newspaper, which is widely acknowledged as the main rival globally for the *Journal*. Rattner says the main reason Murdoch was interested in Pearson was that it owned the *Financial Times*.[5]

However, Murdoch's bid for Dow Jones comes at a time of immense change in the newspaper industry. Advertising sales and circulation revenue have been steadily declining as fewer readers buy print publications from newsstands or pay monthly subscriptions to have them delivered to their home or office.

For this reason, some analysts and investors who follow News Corp. think that now is the time to deemphasize the newspaper publishing business rather than adding on more print publications.

Dow Jones finally agreed to News Corp.'s offer on August 1. At that time, analysts were predicting that Dow Jones' sales in

2008 would increase only 2.4 percent from 2007. So News Corp. was, in essence, buying a company that had very little growth prospects on the immediate horizon.

Of course, Murdoch had a plan. The Dow Jones deal, he has argued, is not about selling newspapers but about generating more and more revenue from Internet advertising. Murdoch bragged that Dow Jones would be able to do a better job of expanding online now that it was a cog in the News Corp. machine than it would on its own as a small family controlled independent firm.

In addition, the acquisition was also clearly made to help bolster the chances of success for News Corp.'s new Fox Business Network, a cable business news network that competes with CNBC, the General Electric–owned network that dominates the cable business news landscape, as well as the smaller Bloomberg Television.

Television insiders had speculated for years that Murdoch would eventually decide to start his own business network. The chatter increased after CNN shut down its CNNfn network in 2004. Murdoch finally made it official in February 2007. In fact, News Corp.'s announcement about the creation of Fox Business Network came on the same day that Murdoch spoke at the McGraw-Hill conference about "cooling" on the idea of buying Dow Jones.

So looking back, it's impossible to separate the decision to buy Dow Jones from the decision to go toe-to-toe with CNBC. Even though CNBC has a contract that runs until 2011, allowing it to share news-gathering resources with the *Wall Street Journal*'s editorial staff, analysts have suggested that the hope is that loyal readers of the *Wall Street Journal* would now become loyal viewers of Fox Business, or, at the very least, make sure to have their TVs tuned to both CNBC and Fox Business during market trading hours.

On the day that Murdoch announced the launch of the network, he was already boasting about how his Fox Business Network would one day supplant CNBC at the top of the ratings. He joked that he was going to keep programming details for the network close to the vest out of fear that CNBC would "immediately copy" Fox.

But Murdoch and other News Corp. executives repeatedly stressed prior to the network's launch in October 2007 that Fox Business would be much different than CNBC, which focused more on day traders and high-level financial news catering to Wall Street junkies. Fox Business, on the other hand, was going to have a more Main Street appeal.

And in August 2007, speaking to shareholders and analysts during an earnings conference call, Murdoch suggested that within "short order" he expected Fox Business Network to be worth about $4 billion, a number that he claimed was about how much CNBC was worth to GE.

These statements are clear signs that Murdoch is not afraid of any challenge. They also show that he obviously thinks every new media property that News Corp. creates is destined not only to dominate its category but in short order to be endlessly copied by the competition. It's an interesting paradox. Murdoch often reminds people in the industry about how he was doubted and how he was viewed as being "crazy." There is a certain degree of defensiveness, a feeling that he still has something to prove to the media world. But at the same time, Murdoch's ego cannot be overstated. Even though he proclaims that people don't take him seriously, he also fully expects that eventually his rivals will mimic him in order to try and duplicate his success.

Time will tell, though, if anyone will ever copy Fox Business. It's been a rough start for the network. According to preliminary figures from Nielsen Media Research, ratings from October 15 through December 14, 2007, the network's first two months on the air, were so low that Nielsen would not disclose the exact numbers.

Nielsen will not report official numbers unless a network reaches a minimum threshold of 35,000 viewers a day on any given weekday. But according to a report in the *New York Times* in January 2008 citing sources who have seen the actual numbers, Fox Business was averaging a scant 6,300 viewers a day compared to 283,000 viewers of CNBC.[6]

Of course, CNBC had an advantage as an established network that is available in more than 90 million homes, while Fox Business was only available in about 30 million homes. Still, the low ratings for Fox Business are surprising in light of the success of the parent network.

Both the Fox News Channel and the Fox broadcast network

aggressively promoted the upcoming debut of Fox Business during commercials in September and early October 2007. The press, in its inimitable way, extensively covered the debut of the channel. There's nothing the mainstream media like to do more than navel-gaze and write about other media companies, even though the average viewer lacks interest in such "inside baseball" topics.

To that end, *Fortune* magazine devoted a lengthy cover story to Fox Business in its October 29, 2007, issue in which it said that "Rupert Murdoch sees FBN as the first step in his strategy to dominate global financial journalism."[7]

It is, of course, premature to proclaim that Fox Business is a failure. And during an earnings conference call in February 2008, both Murdoch and News Corp.'s widely respected president and chief operating officer Peter Chernin maintained that they were happy with the ratings so far and that it was encouraging that the network lost less money than they had budgeted it to lose during its first few months of operations.

Nonetheless, the poor response to Fox Business, as well as increased skepticism of the purchase of Dow Jones (particularly its price), has some followers of Murdoch wondering if he won't eventually wind up parting with Dow Jones and abandoning Fox Business if he grows tired of them.

So, will Dow Jones and Fox Business ultimately meet the same fate as *TV Guide* and the L.A. Dodgers or, like Fox and Fox News, thrive and become flagship franchises for the sprawling media titan?

"There are certain assets that Dow Jones possesses that Murdoch wants to mine for the purposes of expanding his empire, particularly for TV, cable and satellite as well as the Web," said John K. Hartman, a journalism professor at Central Michigan University. "But two or three years down the road, he may decide he no longer needs the entire company. That's his history."[8]

News Corp.'s stock has fallen about 40 percent between the time the Dow Jones deal was announced in May 2007 and July 2008. Shares of all media companies had tumbled in that time frame due to concerns about an economic slowdown in the United States, leading to a pullback in ad dollars as well as consumer spending. So it's not entirely fair to say that News Corp. is being punished by Wall Street solely for the Dow Jones deal.

That said, it's worth noting that shares of one of News Corp.'s biggest competitors, Walt Disney, have held up much better than News Corp. during the same time frame: the Disney stock had fallen about 10 percent.

If News Corp.'s stock continues to suffer, it wouldn't be a big shock to see Murdoch take some action to shake things up. It is his nature to make deals. But it is certainly too soon to declare that Murdoch's Dow Jones gambit is a flop or to expect Murdoch to admit defeat with regard to his financial news aspirations.

"The history of businesspeople trying to compete against Rupert indicates that it's a dumb thing to do," says Larry Haverty, a portfolio manager and analyst with GAMCO Investors, an institutional investment firm that owns more than 14 million shares of News Corp.[9]

Murdoch never has shied away from a fight. And his track record speaks for itself. He has built News Corp. from a mere holding company for the *Adelaide News*, a newspaper he inherited following his father Sir Keith Murdoch's death in 1952, to a global empire with nearly $33 billion in annual revenue that is worth $37 billion. All this and more shows that betting against Murdoch is not a wise decision.

CHAPTER 1

Start Spreading the News

To truly understand just why Murdoch so zealously lusted for Dow Jones, you have to start at the beginning of News Corp.'s history. Today the company is known mainly for its Fox television, cable and movie studios. But News Corp. has always been a newspaper publisher, and Murdoch, despite what his numerous critics maintain, has always considered himself to be an old-fashioned newsman.

Despite the fact that newspaper advertising sales and circulation revenue have been in steady decline for many publishers as more and more readers and marketers flock to the Web, the newspaper business is still a critical one for News Corp.

During the first three quarters of fiscal 2008, which ended in March 2008, News Corp.'s newspaper division accounted for nearly 18 percent of the company's total sales and approximately 13 percent of News Corp.'s operating profits. The importance of the newspaper business to the overall financial picture at News Corp. has increased now that Dow Jones is factored into News Corp.'s results. That deal closed in mid-December 2007.

Rupert Murdoch has given no indication that he would ever get rid of the newspaper business, even though he concedes that the industry faces many daunting challenges. He often has spoken wistfully of the old age of newspapers and has freely admitted that the biggest challenge facing the industry is attracting younger readers, many of whom now get their news solely from the Internet or from "fake news" comedy television shows like the popular *The Daily Show with Jon Stewart* and *The Colbert Report*.

Murdoch clearly still considers himself a newspaperman. It's in his blood, after growing up in the business and taking over the family newspaper business after his father died.

In his remarks at the McGraw-Hill Media Summit in February 2007, Murdoch bemoaned the fact that "the old lifestyle of reading a newspaper over breakfast is gone" and added that the "economics are getting more difficult for newspapers all the time." And in a speech to the American Society of Newspaper Editors in April 2005, Murdoch illustrated the major demographic issues threatening newspaper publishers and conceded that the only way for the industry to survive is that it must adapt to the new habits of younger readers.

"I'm a digital immigrant. I wasn't weaned on the Web, nor coddled on a computer. Instead, I grew up in a highly centralized world where news and information were tightly controlled by a few editors, who deemed to tell us what we could and should know. My two young daughters, on the other hand, will be digital natives. They'll never know a world without ubiquitous broadband Internet access," he said, referring to his two girls from his third marriage, Grace and Chloe, who were toddlers at the time.

The news industry has transformed to one where individual bloggers and readers have as much say, if not more, than editors, publishers and large media conglomerates in dictating the flow of news coverage. This is a far cry from the way the industry was run in the early 1950s.

Rupert Murdoch served an apprenticeship at the *Melbourne Herald* in 1949, and while attending Oxford University in England he spent summers working at publications in London's Fleet Street news district.

Following Sir Keith Murdoch's death in 1952, much of his company's assets were sold to pay debts. Rupert, however, assumed control of the *Adelaide News*, which he began running in 1954, and over the next few years he built up a portfolio of Australian newspapers and television stations to turn his company, then known as News Limited, into a major media player in his native country. (News Limited changed its name to News Corporation in 1980.)

By 1960, Murdoch had acquired a stake in the Perth *Sunday Times*, television station Channel 9 in Adelaide, the women's magazine *New Idea* and, most notably, the *Daily Mirror* in Sydney. In 1964, Murdoch launched his first new publication, the national paper the *Australian*. News Limited also acquired a stake in Wellington Publishing, the largest media firm in New Zealand, that year.

But this was obviously only the beginning, as Murdoch soon set his sights on two markets with far more growth potential than Australia—Britain and the United States.

In 1969, Murdoch made his first move to establish a beachhead in the United Kingdom, beating out Czech-born media titan Robert Maxwell in a bidding war for *News of the World*. The publication, a more-than-a-century-old popular British weekly tabloid known for its cheeky coverage of scandals and crime, was highly sought after by both moguls.

And with that deal, it appears that Murdoch's zeal for making acquisitions, especially when he could outspend someone else, was born.

"He always wants to do deals. It's his raison d'être. He has outfoxed, no pun intended, a host of notable and very successful competitors going all the way back to beating out Maxwell for *News of the World*. He lusts for deals and he is a visionary," says Richard Dorfman, managing director of Richard Alan Inc., an investment company focused on the media industry and based in New York.[1]

Later that year, Murdoch also acquired the *Sun*. Under Murdoch, the paper quickly became a controversial staple of the

British media scene. In 1969, the *Sun* began running photos of female models on its third page, a feature created to help the *Sun* compete with its top rival, the *Daily Mirror*, which typically ran pinup photos of women in bikinis or lingerie.

But after a few months, the *Sun* upped the ante and ran its first topless photo of a female model on the third page, an attention-grabbing ploy that immediately led to an increase in sales for the *Sun*. It was the beginning of a Murdoch trend, one that has made him the target of many in the media industry who disapprove of his style of journalism. Murdoch simply took a page, so to speak, from a competitor, and went even further with it. It was a prime example of Murdoch marrying sensationalism and entertainment with news in order to sell more papers. And it's a tactic that he is still using today. The "Page 3 girl" remains a daily feature in the *Sun*, and the women are still topless.

Murdoch and the *Sun* have been criticized by many in Britain for the feature, which has been dubbed as sexist. Still, the current editor of the *Sun*, Rebekah Wade, defended the "Page 3 girl" in testimony to the House of Lords Select Committee on Communications in January 2008 as part of an ongoing Parliament inquiry into media ownership in the United Kingdom. Wade, who has been editor of the *Sun* since 2003 and before that was the editor of *News of the World*, said she did not deem the feature to be sexist.

"Our *Sun* readers love it—both male and female *Sun* readers," she said during her testimony, adding later that "there cannot be many people in the country who do not know that the Page 3 girls are on page 3 of the *Sun* every day."[2]

When asked if she thought sales would drop if the paper dropped the Page 3 feature, Wade responded that "it is an interesting question. I have no idea what would happen. I love Page 3 and so I would not drop it, but I do not know what would happen."[3]

The *Sun's* rise to prominence in Britain—thanks to the allure of the naked female breast—marked a turning point in the news industry, and all of Murdoch's newspapers worldwide followed suit. They all hyped the sex and sleaze factor in order to boost newsstand sales and circulation.

By the mid-1970s, Murdoch was looking to emulate his success in Britain in the United States. In 1972, News Limited acquired its first newspapers in America, purchasing the *San Antonio Express* and the *San Antonio News* from U.S. media firm Harte-Hanks. The *San Antonio News* had a style similar to the tabloids until the two papers were merged to form the *San Antonio Express-News* in 1984.

Establishing a printing operation in the United States was a crucial step for Murdoch that would help him expand further in America. In 1974, News Limited launched a weekly supermarket tabloid called the *National Star*, which was meant to compete directly against the leader in this niche, the *National Enquirer*. The *National Star*, later known as just the *Star*, was often printed on News Limited's San Antonio presses. And the publication, despite facing an uphill battle against a dominant market leader, quickly became an equal to the *National Enquirer*. By the early 1980s, the *Star's* circulation was nearly equal to the *National Enquirer's*, according to an analysis by the Project for Excellence in Journalism, a research organization affiliated with the Pew Charitable Trusts.

However, it was Murdoch's purchase of the *New York Post* that would help make him a household name far beyond the borders of Australia and the United Kingdom. In 1976, News Limited bought the *Post*, which proudly bore the stamp of founder Alexander Hamilton on its front page. The paper was famous for being an extremely liberal publication under long-time owner Dorothy Schiff. The *Post* quickly established a much more conservative editorial bent, though, to the consternation of many Democrats.

It also, like its tabloid brethren in the United Kingdom, acquired a taste for the sensational. And for better or for worse—and many within the media industry would vociferously argue that it's the latter—the *New York Post* and Murdoch's British tabloids have irrevocably changed the business. The witty headlines and salacious gossip found in the *Sun* and the *New York Post* helped set the stage for the unceasing celebrity "news" coverage of the latter part of the twentieth century and early twenty-first century.

The famous 1982 headline in the *New York Post*, "Headless Body in Topless Bar," became such a popular part of the cultural zeitgeist that in many newsrooms today it is still uttered with mixed feelings of disdain and grudging respect. The headline even wound up being fodder for a cheesy low-budget movie of the same name in 1995.

Television shows like *Inside Edition* and *Access Hollywood* and Web sites such as PerezHilton.com and TMZ.com certainly owe a debt of gratitude to Murdoch, since it is debatable whether there would be a celebrity gossip industry if not for the likes of the *New York Post's* ubiquitous Page 6 feature.

The *New York Post* has never been a big earner for News Corp. In fact, most analysts believe it continues to bleed red ink to this day. But Murdoch has had such a fascination with the tabloid that he has bought it twice. In 1988, Murdoch was forced to sell the paper due to pressure from the U.S. government. Some politicians frowned on him owning a newspaper and television station in the same market. However, Murdoch was able to convince the Federal Communications Commission to grant News Corp. a new waiver in 1993 that allowed the company to own both the *New York Post* and local New York television station and Fox affiliate WNYW. This allowed Murdoch to rescue the paper from financial ruin. It was on the verge of being shut down.

This would not be Murdoch's last foray into the United States either. He acquired the famously liberal alternative weekly the *Village Voice* in 1977, the tabloid the *Boston Herald American*, later renamed the *Boston Herald*, in 1982 and the tabloid *Chicago Sun-Times* in 1983.

But it was the *New York Post*, thanks to its presence in the world's media capital, that helped to establish Murdoch as a celebrity in his own right. However, with his increased fame came increased scrutiny. Murdoch's empire grew, and as it did, so did the number of critics. It seemed as if Murdoch, a lightning rod for controversy, was constantly under fire for one reason or another, and the media seldom missed a chance to take a shot at him when the opportunity presented itself.

While the cheeky tone of News Corp.'s tabloids had raised some eyebrows due to questions of poor taste, the ritualistic building up and tearing down of celebrities in publications like the *Sun* and the *New York Post* were considered relatively harmless. What did cause a ruckus among media followers, particularly those with a more liberal bent, was that Murdoch often used his news operations to influence public policy.

Dorfman said he found this criticism to be a little unfair. He thinks that at the end of the day Murdoch's motivation for owning newspapers is profits first and politics second.

"When Murdoch takes over companies and puts his crews in there, especially with publishing, he gets a bad rep for being a conservative-leaning monster. But he's not buying things just to propagate his conservative message," Dorfman said. "Yes, he does have a conservative ideology. A lot of people were upset when Murdoch took over the *New York Post* and he turned it from a reasonably serious paper into a tabloid. But he made it a more viable entity. When people go off about him bringing in ideological brethren and saying that he's an ogre, I think that's completely unfair. He's there to make money."[4]

Nonetheless, it's hard to deny that Murdoch's papers have more often than not been reflections of his political views. For example, the *New York Post*, while a more viable entity under Murdoch than it was before he acquired it for the first time in 1976, has never been a major profit source. This begs the question: Why has his infatuation with newspapers remained undiminished for so long, given the realities of their business model? Why has he accumulated more and more newspapers even while readership the world over has been drying up?

This became a more pointed question when Murdoch acquired a British newspaper with a far more solid editorial reputation than *News of the World*, the *Sun* and the *New York Post*. In 1981, Murdoch acquired the *Times* and *Sunday Times* from Thomson Corp. These publications were considered to be among the most highbrow in Britain, competing with other "serious" papers such as the *Observer* and the *Guardian*. The coverage of British politics in Murdoch's papers, particularly the loyal support for Margaret Thatcher and the Conservative Party in the 1980s and criticism of the European Economic and Monetary Union in the 1990s, were routinely attacked by those who felt Murdoch's editors and writers were being forced to parrot Murdoch's beliefs.

Murdoch addressed some of the concerns about his influence during a meeting with members of the House of Lords Select Committee on Communications in New York in September 2007. He gave a candid, and at times unapologetic, view of his role in shaping news coverage.

According to the minutes from that meeting, Murdoch said that he felt the media's main role was "to inform." But the minutes went on to note that Murdoch "did not disguise the fact that he is hands-on both economically and editorially." Murdoch told Parliament members that "the law" does not allow him to instruct the editors of the *Times* and the *Sunday Times* and added that there is an independent editorial board in place to ensure that he does not interfere with editorial news judgment.[5]

But Murdoch went on to admit that while he never tells editors to specifically "do this or that," he often asks, "What are you doing?" He added that he sees a difference between his role at the *Times* and the *Sunday Times* and how he may influence editorial coverage at his tabloids the *Sun* and *News of the World*. Likewise, he said he felt the same way about how he ran the *New York Post* and how he would run the *Wall Street Journal* once that became a part of News Corp.[6]

For the tabloids, Murdoch described himself as a "traditional proprietor." And the minutes noted that Murdoch "exercises editorial control on major issues—like which Party to back in a general election or policy on Europe."[7]

Current and former high-ranking editorial employees from Murdoch's British newspapers confirmed that Murdoch has had a high degree of influence over editorial decisions at both the tabloids and the more highly regarded *Times* and *Sunday Times*.

During her testimony to the House of Lords in January 2008, Wade would not go as far as to say that Murdoch gave her direct instructions about how to cover stories in either the *Sun* or *News of the World*. But she made no secret of the fact that some of her political views mirrored Murdoch's, which was probably a major reason why she was named editor of the two publications in the first place. The admission certainly gives some insight as to how politics do enter into Murdoch's thinking when making decisions about editorial personnel. Clearly, it is important to him to hire people who share his political views. In that regard, he can avoid making overt requests regarding editorial coverage since he already knows that his handpicked editor is likely to deliver a headline and story that he will approve.

Rebekah Wade expanded on this point: "It would be fair to say that I have worked for Mr. Murdoch for eighteen years and twelve of those years I have either been a deputy editor or an editor. I think it would be fair to say that, before any appointment, he knew me pretty well—any senior appointment. In that way, he would be aware of my views, both social views, cultural views and political views."[8]

To that end, Wade said that she, like Murdoch, was adamantly opposed to both the notion of a unified Europe and the idea of Britain joining the European Union. And Murdoch was criticized by many in Europe for letting his anti-EU bias be expressed through his newspapers.

"Take Europe for example—that is quite a good one to bring up—Mr. Murdoch was absolutely aware of my views on Europe, I think even before I became editor of the *News of the World*, maybe even deputy editor. I am very strongly against a federal Europe and the bureaucracy that it creates, and I think that it is hugely damaging to my readers' lives. I am very, very strong on that; probably, in some ways, much stronger than Mr. Murdoch's own opinion. So the European campaign absolutely comes from me," she said.[9]

She added that she did consult with Murdoch in 2005 about the *Sun*'s coverage of the election in Britain that year—the paper wound up endorsing Prime Minister and Labor Party leader Tony Blair. "I did talk to Mr. Murdoch of course. Mr. Murdoch is a lifelong newspaperman; he has also lived through political change both here and in America and Australia; his advice is always exemplary and good," she said.[10]

However, after a series of questions about just how involved Murdoch was in the day-to-day operations of the *Sun*, Wade downplayed how much she actually is in contact with Murdoch. "Mr. Murdoch runs a global media company with vast interests all around the world. He travels all the time. He is a very hands-on, not 'proprietor,' but he is very hands-on in the way he runs his business, which is why it is so successful. So the idea that I talk to him about everything is inconceivable," she said.[11]

But Andrew Neil, a former editor of the *Sunday Times* for eleven years, also testified that Murdoch had a very hands-on approach to coverage at that more prestigious publication, despite the fact that there was an independent board that prevented him from specifically "instructing" editors what to do and not do.

"I think the key word in Mr. Murdoch's sentence there is 'instruct.' He does not instruct the quality newspaper editors of the *Times* and the *Sunday Times*, but that does not mean to say that he does not have influence and he does not let you know what he thinks. There are many ways in which you can influence a newspaper without giving a downright instruction. Throughout the eleven years that I was editor of the *Sunday Times*, I never got an instruction to take a particular line, I never got an instruction to put something on the front page and I do not think I even got an instruction not to do something, but I was never left in any doubt what he wanted," Neil said.[12]

When asked for further clarification about how Neil would know exactly what Murdoch wanted, Neil said, "Because you would get periodic telephone calls, sometimes they would come fast and furious, at other times you would not hear from him at all, and, in every discussion you had with him, he let you know his views. On every major issue of the time and every major political personality or business personality, I knew what he thought and you knew, as an editor, that you did not have a freehold, you had a leasehold, as editor, and that leasehold depended on accommodating his views in most cases, not all cases, and there were sometimes quite serious disagreements we had and I still survived as editor. I have always said that to survive with Rupert Murdoch, indeed any proprietor, an editor has to be on the same planet. You do not necessarily have to be on the same continent or even in the same country all the time, but you have to be on the same planet, otherwise the relationship does not work."[13]

Neil, like Wade, mentioned that he also had views similar to Murdoch's, which was probably a reason he was able to work for Murdoch as long as he did. He joked during this testimony that Murdoch knew when he first hired Neil that he "did not have a background in the Socialist Workers' Revolutionary Party."[14]

But Neil painted a picture of Murdoch that indicated he was far more of a control freak and micromanager than Wade did. "He does not regard himself as Editor-in-Chief of the *Times* or the *Sunday Times*, but he does regard himself as someone who should have more influence on these papers than anybody else, and part of the process of him letting you know his mind, in addition to calls and conversations, is to clip out editorials from, above all, the *Wall Street Journal* because he loved the *Wall Street Journal*, and he will love it even more now that he owns it, and he would clip out editorials and he would fax them over to you, in the days of the fax, and that was a clear indication that it would not be a bad idea to take this editorial line. I used to get them on Star Wars, on Reagan, on the Cold War and so on, and sometimes you followed them and sometimes you did not," Neil said.[15]

Neil also took issue with Wade's characterization of Murdoch as someone who was not terribly interested in what was in the *Sun* or other tabloids beyond their entertainment news.

Wade said that one of the biggest disagreements Murdoch has had with her is that "Mr. Murdoch is often dismayed by the amount of celebrity coverage I put in my newspaper, particularly on *Big Brother* for example," she said, referring to the popular British reality television show. "He cannot understand why I devote so many pages to *Big Brother*," she said, before adding, when pressed about any other major bones of contention she's had with Murdoch, "*I'm a Celebrity, Get Me Out of Here* often can cause problems too; whereas we absolutely are in agreement on *Pop Idol*, and he thinks that is very good. You know, it is serious stuff here!"[16]

In other words, Wade tried to paint a picture of Murdoch as a serious newsman whose only cause for concern was that his tabloids had too many stories about frivolous reality television shows like *I'm a Celebrity* and *Pop Idol*. She denied that Murdoch was playing a role in dictating political coverage.

However, Neil said, "Although he is not named as Editor-in-Chief of the *Sun* or the *News of the World*, that is, in reality, what he is. There is no major political position the *Sun* will take, whether it is attitude to the euro or to the current European Treaty or to whom the paper will support in the upcoming general election; none of that can be decided without Rupert Murdoch's major input." Neil also indicated that when he worked for the *Sun*, the editor "would get daily telephone calls. I was lucky, I only got them once or twice a week, sometimes once a month, but Kelvin MacKenzie, when he was editor, would have daily conversations, not to determine what the headline was going to be on the front page or exactly what it would be, but to make sure that on every major issue, and of course in those days the *Sun* was a far more influential newspaper in the politics of this land than it is now, it followed the Rupert Murdoch line."[17]

And confirming perhaps what most Murdoch critics had feared, Neil further claimed in his testimony that since the *Sun* was taken over by News Limited in 1969, "it has never taken a position at an election that did not have the full-hearted support and, indeed, it was because of the full-hearted influence of Rupert Murdoch."[18]

It is apparent from the comments of both Neil and Wade that Murdoch can very easily get the type of coverage he wants from his newspapers. Sometimes Murdoch may have to be more of a micromanager and make direct calls to and demands of his editors. But very often editors seem to already know exactly what Murdoch wants to see. So decisions are made in order to make sure the editors are not on the receiving end of a Murdoch call asking, "What are you doing?" Either way, if Murdoch is explicitly helping craft editorial coverage through specific demands or if editors are simply doing what they believe he will want them to do so they can avoid incurring his wrath, the results are the same. The coverage in Murdoch-owned newspapers indelibly bears the stamp of Murdoch's political views.

Nonetheless, even though Neil had a falling out with Murdoch and left the *Sunday Times* in 1996 to write for rival the *Daily*

Mail, Neil ultimately defended in his testimony Murdoch's right to act as he has done throughout the years. Neil is now the chairman of Press Holdings Media Group, publisher of the conservative magazine *The Spectator*.

"When this debate takes place in Britain, it often precedes what, I think, is a rather bizarre assumption that the person who owns the newspaper, puts up the capital to buy it, takes all the risks, pays the bills and deals with any fallout that an editor gets up to, including massive libel bills, should be the one person that should have no say over the content of the newspaper, and that just seems to me to be bizarre," Neil said. "That is very different from saying that the proprietor should edit the newspaper; that is a different matter. The idea that a proprietor should have no say on the direction of content of the newspaper seems to me to be crazy. After all, frankly that person surely has more right to a say than anybody else in the land other than the editor."[19]

So even though it may be tempting to dismiss Neil's comments as nothing more than sour grapes from a disgruntled former employee, it would be unwise to do so. Instead, Neil's comments, combined with Wade's testimony as well as Murdoch's own remarks during his conversation with House of Lords members, should be interpreted as perhaps the most relevant insight into the thought process behind Murdoch's assembling of his newspaper empire and what Murdoch's motives truly are. This examination of Murdoch's admittedly active role with his newspapers does come at an uncomfortable time for

News Corp., since it coincides with the consummation of the Dow Jones acquisition. Because of that acquisition, many in the media are scrutinizing Murdoch even more closely for any whiff of interference in Dow Jones' coverage of China, a market that, as will be discussed in more detail later on, has become an area of intense focus for Murdoch and all of News Corp.

But perhaps an even bigger concern for Murdoch and News Corp. should not be whether Dow Jones' legacy risks being tarnished by guilty association with Murdoch but whether News Corp. really should continue to be such a big player in the newspaper industry. As Murdoch has pointed out, newspapers are no longer a high-growth industry. And even though News Corp. boldly decided to place a bigger bet on the industry with the Dow Jones purchase, the newspaper business has been diminishing in prominence for News Corp. during the past few decades.

News Corp. has shed nearly all of its American-based publications in order either to help finance growth opportunities in other businesses or in response to the financial crisis in the early 1990s that nearly crippled News Corp.

Murdoch sold the *Village Voice* in 1985 and the *Chicago Sun-Times* in 1986. At the time, News Corp. was preparing to launch the Fox television network in the United States. It also sold many of the travel trade magazines it had acquired in 1984 from Ziff Davis for $350 million to Reed International in 1989 for $825 million.

In 1990, with the company having to face looming debt-related problems, News Corp. sold *Star* to the *National Enquirer's* parent company. In 1993, News Corp. unloaded the merged *San Antonio Express-News*, and a year later the *Boston Herald* was sold off as well.

However, News Corp. did make two other small newspaper acquisitions in 2006 to complement the *New York Post.* Murdoch bought the *Times Ledger* and *Courier-Life*—two community newspaper chains that publish weekly newspapers predominantly in the New York City boroughs of Brooklyn and Queens. Despite those purchases, News Corp. remained largely in retrenchment mode until the Dow Jones deal.

So how much longer can Murdoch continue to embrace his first business love? The newspaper business has changed to the point where in an increasingly fragmented media world, the reader has more choices and more power as well.

Many younger readers flocking to the Web no longer want their news from mainstream media sources, a development that Murdoch begrudgingly admitted during his remarks to House of Lords committee members in September 2007.

"You have to throw it all out there and trust the public. Who are we to say what they can choose?" he said about the rise of blogs and how that has added to the "sheer chaotic mass of material out there."[20]

But beyond the demographic issues, there are other major problems plaguing the industry.

"There are tremendous fixed costs, such as the price of gasoline, which affects distribution costs, that newspaper companies have no control over," said Central Michigan University journalism professor John Hartman, adding that on top of that there are also obvious big costs for newsprint and paper.[21]

Murdoch has taken steps to address the cost issue. In 2004, following the lead of other prominent British newspapers, the *Times of London* went from being printed as a broadsheet, a style of newspaper featuring long vertical pages that typically is associated with more prestigious newspapers, to the more compact tabloid style that was used by Murdoch's other British newspapers. The change helped lead to lower printing expenses and also a boost in sales.

But Murdoch conceded in February 2007 at the McGraw-Hill media conference that cutting costs could only go so far as a means to boost profits, and added that at a time when more and more news sources were free of charge on the Web, newspapers could not count on raising newspaper prices to help lift margins either.

"Increasing the price hurts your circulation and additional cost cutting is not the right approach," Murdoch said.

Complicating matters, if Murdoch suddenly had a change of heart and decided that the time was right for News Corp. to either further scale back in the newspaper business or completely turn back on its newspaper roots and exit the industry entirely, the company would probably have a tough time finding many willing buyers for its newspapers.

"We look at a lot of newspaper deals but they are not easy to complete," said Quadrangle's Steven Rattner in October 2007 about interest in the newspaper business from his firm and other private equity investors. "This industry is under a fair amount of operating pressure. It's risky to make an investment in companies on a downward trajectory."[22]

Murdoch seems to realize this and he has discussed the eventual need for the newspaper industry to eliminate the "paper" part of the business. While giving the annual lecture at the Worshipful Company of Stationers and Newspaper Makers, a prominent trade organization in London, in March 2006, Murdoch said that even though he thought "traditional newspapers have many years of life left . . . in the future that newsprint and ink will be just one of many channels to our readers."[23]

He concluded, "What happens to print journalism in an age where consumers are increasingly being offered on-demand, interactive, news, entertainment, sport and classifieds via broadband on their computer screens, TV screens, mobile phones and handsets? The answer is that great journalism will always attract readers. The words, pictures and graphics that are the stuff of journalism have to be brilliantly packaged; they must feed the mind and move the heart. And, crucially, newspapers must give readers a choice of accessing their journalism in the pages of the paper or on websites such as Times Online or—and this is important—on any platform that appeals to them, mobile phones, hand-held devices, iPods, whatever. As I have said newspapers may become news-sites."[24]

With that in mind, industry observers say that Murdoch's next move in the news business beyond Dow Jones could be to buy more news-related Web sites and eschew more print publications.

"There is anxiety about the future of print. So far, digital sales are not replacing the lost print ad revenues. The most likely scenario for News Corp. is that they'll hunker down and focus on the digital strategy and buy more online assets. The *Journal* is probably the last paper Murdoch will buy for awhile," said Reed Phillips, managing partner with DeSilva & Phillips, a media investment bank based in New York.[25]

But News Corp. also announced in 2004 that it was investing in new color printing plants over the next four to five years in Britain, a sign that Murdoch hasn't completely given up on the dead-tree variety of selling news.

"At News Corporation we have always been a long-term investor at the forefront of technological innovation. This exciting new project demonstrates again our absolute commitment to the future of print," Murdoch said at the time.[26]

Nonetheless, if the newspaper businesses continue to lose readers and ad revenue and post uninspiring profit margins, Murdoch could face pressure from shareholders to exit the business entirely.

Many Wall Street institutional investors have begun to shun newspaper publishers and companies with significant exposure to the moribund newspaper industry because of the industry's slow-growth characteristics. Newspaper stocks have plunged during the past few years; despite this, many savvy investors still don't think it's the right time to buy.

The stocks might seem "cheap," but just because the stocks have already fallen sharply does not mean they won't fall even further. "We might look to buy some newspaper stocks on a value basis but we typically move to where the action is in the market and there's not a whole lot of action in that industry," said Craig Hodges, comanager of the Dallas-based Hodges Fund in September 2007.[27]

What's more, other newspaper publishers are deciding that it is time to spin off their newspaper operations into separately traded companies. In February 2008, local television station owner Belo Corp. spun off A. H. Belo, which owns the *Dallas Morning News*, the *Providence Journal* and several other newspapers.

And E. W. Scripps plans to make a similar move. The company—which owns newspapers such as the *Rocky Mountain News* in Denver and the *Commercial Appeal* in Memphis, as well as local TV stations, the cable networks Food Network and HGTV and the online comparison shopping site Shopzilla—said in October 2007 that it plans to create a new company. It will be called Scripps Networks Interactive, which will own all of Scripps' cable TV and Internet assets.

The company that will retain the E. W. Scripps name will hold on to the newspapers, local TV stations and United Media, which syndicates popular comics such as *Peanuts* and *Dilbert*. E. W. Scripps' chief operating officer, Richard Boehne, who will become the CEO of the newspaper and television part of Scripps following the company's split, said when announcing the spin-off that the past twenty-four months for the newspaper business have been among the toughest ever for the industry, due to the increased competition from the Internet.

Despite this, Murdoch has shown no signs that he is looking to scale back his newspaper holdings. He claims to have the right mix of newspaper assets that can successfully make the transition to the Web.

"Our print businesses, and especially newspapers—the historic heart of this company—continue to deliver value for our company and shareholders, in part by generating huge amounts of cash that fund and fulfill our strategy. Right now our print businesses have more total readers than they ever have, thanks to the Internet. The distinction that today seems to divide 'new' and 'old' media will prove illusory over time. In the meantime, we are investing in the future of these businesses," Murdoch said in his annual address to shareholders in October 2006.[28]

But many in the media business and on Wall Street do not share this vision.

"The halcyon era of newspapers is long gone," said Scott Black, president of Delphi Management, a Boston-based institutional investment firm, in September 2007. Black owns stakes in News Corp. and the Washington Post Company, but he said he is a bigger fan of News Corp.'s other assets and that he doesn't even consider Washington Post Company a newspaper company anymore since it generates a sizable amount of sales and profits from its Kaplan educational business.[29]

Fortunately for News Corp., it is much more than a newspaper company. So it is not as threatened by the seismic shifts taking place in media as much as pure-play print competitors such as the *New York Times*, Gannett and McClatchy are. Murdoch, despite his sentimental attachment to the newspaper business, has been savvy and unemotional enough to cut ties with some newspaper assets when he needed to dedicate cash elsewhere. And even when News Corp. was busy in the 1980s making a bigger name for itself on Madison Avenue and Fleet Street, Murdoch never lost sight of an even bigger goal for his company—cracking the Hollywood elite. In the mid-1980s, News Corp. would make an acquisition that was undoubtedly the most significant one in the company's history at that time and is arguably, more than two decades later, still the smartest move that Murdoch ever made.

CHAPTER 2

Crazy Like a Fox

I t is difficult to imagine what News Corp. would look like today if Murdoch did not decide in 1985 to acquire TCF Holdings, the parent company of the venerable 20th Century Fox
movie studio.

The purchase set the stage for News Corp. to become one of
the leading players in the entertainment industry, an area of the
media far more exalted, not to mention more lucrative, than
newspaper and book publishing, News Corp.'s "traditional"
media assets.

In the first nine months of fiscal 2008, News Corp.'s filmed
entertainment unit boasted operating profit margins of 20 percent and the television division's margins were 19 percent. By
way of comparison, News Corp.'s book publishing unit Harper-
Collins had operating margins of 13 percent, while margins in
the cutthroat newspaper business were only 11 percent. Overall,

News Corp.'s operating profit margins in the first three quarters of fiscal 2008 were 16 percent.

This trend continues. During the first nine months of fiscal 2008, News Corp. generated 21 percent of its total sales and more than a quarter of its operating profits from its filmed entertainment division and 18 percent of revenue and 20 percent of operating profits from its television business, which includes Asia's STAR network in addition to Fox in the United States.

It's easy to say now that buying Fox was a brilliant move and huge success for Murdoch. The Fox movie studio has been directly responsible for several of the biggest box office blockbusters of the past two decades, including the three *Star Wars* prequels, *Independence Day*, *Home Alone* and *Night at the Museum*, and was a coproducer with Paramount on *Titanic*, the all-time box office champ in the United States. What's more, the Fox broadcast network has topped the ratings race in the 18- to 49-year-old demographic, the age group most highly sought after by advertisers, from 2004 through 2008 thanks to hit dramas such as *House* and *24*, its long-running animated show *The Simpsons* and the colossal ratings juggernaut known as *American Idol*.

But when Murdoch first disclosed his plans to become a Hollywood mogul in 1985, there were groans of skepticism and questions about whether Murdoch had lost his mind. In March 1985, News Corp. announced it was buying 50 percent of 20th Century Fox from American oil baron Marvin Davis for $250 million. The deal was made as the Fox studio was reeling following several box office duds. In addition, Fox was deep in debt. In fact, as part of News Corp.'s investment, Murdoch agreed to advance $88 million to 20th Century Fox for immediate use to pay down debt.

The purchase of Fox gave Murdoch a foray into the film and television distribution businesses, assets that would help provide programming for his fledgling broadcasting operations in Australia and Britain. But this was not the first time that Murdoch tried to buy his way into the film and television market. In 1984, he threatened to wage a hostile takeover for control of Warner Communications. Murdoch had amassed a 5.6 percent stake in Warner and was seeking to buy up to 50 percent. He eventually walked away from a proxy fight and agreed to sell his stake back to Warner for $173 million. Warner would later merge with Time Inc. and that combined company would eventually buy Turner Broadcasting Systems before merging with AOL to create what is now known as Time Warner.

Murdoch's purchase of a 50 percent stake in Fox also came at a time when consolidation was heating up throughout the media business, particularly in television and movies. Just a few days earlier, television and radio station owner Capital Cities Communications Inc. announced it had agreed to buy the American Broadcasting Company, owner of the ABC television network, for $3.5 billion. (Disney would later buy Capital Cities.) Murdoch clearly saw value in the company, but many media observers were confused by why Murdoch wanted an asset that was clearly troubled.

"This is a significant investment for News Corp.," Murdoch

said in a statement. "Twentieth Century-Fox is one of the world's few great film and television companies, and ... is positioning itself for significant growth."

The purchase was yet another example of Murdoch's revelation that in order for News Corp. to be a truly global player in the media business, he had to expand beyond the stodgy world of newspapers. Content, as the well-worn cliché in the media world goes, is king. Murdoch knew that News Corp. could not truly become a competitor with other media conglomerates like Disney and Warner Communications unless he, too, had a significant stake in Hollywood.

However, Lee Isgur, an analyst with Wall Street firm Paine Webber, which has since been acquired by Swiss bank UBS, told the *New York Times* after the Fox deal was announced that Murdoch "likes the idea of having a film library and a production arm" and that "if he can have 20th Century's film library and distribution rights, that's not bad." He also viewed Murdoch's motivation for the purchase as being more than financially driven. "He's also got an ego, and he wants to get into the business," Isgur added.[1]

Still, this was just a small sign of what was to come from Murdoch. He would not be content owning a mere 50 percent of a film and television production company. In order to make his gamble on content pay off, he needed more outlets to air his programming as well. News Corp. owned the Nine Network in Australia, one of that country's largest television networks, and had acquired the popular Sky Network in Britain in 1983. News

Corp. was starting to experiment with the idea of launching full-blown satellite television networks in the United Kingdom and America. But Murdoch still did not have enough distribution outlets to justify the Fox deal. That would soon change.

Less than two months after announcing the 50 percent stake in Fox, Murdoch struck again, agreeing in May to team up with Marvin Davis to buy six local U.S. television stations from American media firm Metromedia for $1.5 billion. In order to cinch the deal, Murdoch was forced to give up his Australian citizenship and become a U.S. citizen so that he would comply with Federal Communications Commission laws that prevented foreigners from owning U.S. television stations.

The purchase of the Metromedia stations was hailed by some as the creation of the first global media empire, since it gave Murdoch ownership of broadcast assets on three continents. The deal led to speculation that Murdoch, along with Barry Diller, the veteran Hollywood executive who joined Fox in 1984 to lead its television studio programming, might use the combination of the Fox studio and the local television stations to launch a fourth network to rival the established ABC, CBS and NBC networks.

It was a stunningly bold idea, and Murdoch and Diller would confirm just a few months later that this was their plan. But before that, some media rivals wondered whether Murdoch paid too much for the Metromedia stations. In hindsight these comments are amusing when you consider how much of a financial boon Fox has been to News Corp.

Over the next few decades, Murdoch would continue to pay lofty sums for other media companies. And despite his numerous successes, skeptics would continue to question if he was spending too much for them. So it's interesting to look back at how many industry experts thought Murdoch was out of his mind for spending as much as he did for the Metromedia stations.

"It's a very, very pricey deal," one media executive who asked not to be named told the *Washington Post* in May 1985. "It's tough to get any real world numbers for justification of the deal. The size of the deal must presume that a very significant premium has been paid—implicitly for the potential as well as explicitly for the cash flow. The potential is mainly the chance to build a fourth network—which is a nice idea on the blackboard, but he'd have to make a significant additional commitment requiring a lot more deficit spending. It is a very defensible acquisition for strategic reasons, but on economic terms … no matter what numbers you use, you can't figure out how this whole thing hangs together."[2]

A television executive, who also spoke to the *Washington Post* on the condition of anonymity, openly scoffed at the $1.5 billion price tag because Murdoch was only buying a handful of stations, while Capital Cities was paying $3.5 billion to acquire an entire network in ABC.

"Murdoch paid two-thirds of what Capital Cities paid for a network that was already in place," said the television executive. "In my estimation, they probably made a bad buy." The network executive went on to add that "Murdoch is the guy who is running the *New York Post* at a $10 million a year loss because he wants to have a newspaper in New York."[3]

Murdoch, not surprisingly, was undeterred by the criticism and defended the purchase price because the deal gave him stations in three of the biggest U.S. markets: New York, Chicago and Los Angeles.

"When one considers the markets, I don't think the price was expensive at all. There just had to be a premium. But remember that we got some of the biggest markets in the world in one swoop," Murdoch said in an interview with the *Washington Post*.[4]

The risk that Murdoch was taking with the Metromedia stations would soon expand, raising yet more questions as to whether News Corp. was mortgaging its future on a quixotic quest in an attempt to do something that no one in America thought was a wise idea. It seemed Murdoch was trying to belly up to the television network table, demanding a full serving of the lucrative television advertising revenue pie instead of just settling for some crumbs from the established giants.

Murdoch's partnership with Davis quickly fizzled after the two agreed to buy the Metromedia stations, meaning that News Corp. was now on tap to foot the entire $1.5 billion price. What's more, Murdoch completed his acquisition of Fox in September 1985, agreeing to buy out Davis's remaining 50 percent stake in TCF for $325 million. The end of the relationship with Davis should not have come as a huge surprise, since Murdoch clearly is not someone who is happy with being a mere co-owner in a joint venture. At the very least, if he can't own something outright, he wants a controlling interest. And with Davis out of the picture, the rewards from Fox and Metromedia were now fully set to be consumed by Murdoch. But with that, he had to assume a lot more of the potential financial downside.

With the completion of the TCF purchase, Murdoch had now committed, in the span of just six months, $2.075 billion to acquire Fox and a half dozen local television stations. Since Murdoch had yet to announce the launch of the Fox television network, puzzled analysts wondered what the endgame was. Many questioned whether it really was worth spending more than $2 billion just so Murdoch could boast that he was a true global media baron. Or was there an actual plan in place to take advantage of his newfound clout in Hollywood? The industry would only have to wait a few more weeks for the answer.

On October 9, 1985, Murdoch forever changed the television and media landscape in the United States when News Corp. formally announced plans to use the television stations from Metromedia as the base to launch a fourth broadcast network in the United States. The Fox Broadcasting Company, as it was to be known, was going to be led by Diller, whom Murdoch promoted to chairman and CEO of TCF, giving him control of the television and movie studios as well as the six local networks that News Corp. was buying from Metromedia.

Murdoch had little to say about the launch on the day of the announcement, but he had been dropping hints ever since amassing the initial 50 percent stake in Fox that he eventually wanted to start a fourth network. But in describing his reason for making the bet on movies and television in an interview in *Folio* magazine earlier in 1985, Murdoch said that it was simply the right time to react to the rapidly changing landscape in the media business. In other words, instead of spending a lot of time staring at the pieces on the media chessboard and studiously analyzing how every decision would play out over the long haul, Murdoch felt that quick, decisive action was needed.

"A lot of people claim they have ten-year plans or five-year plans or something. But basically, the most successful businesses are opportunistic and you take your opportunities when they come," Murdoch said in the *Folio* interview.[5]

Those are words that Murdoch would continue to live by as he made more and more acquisitions in the years and decades to come. Sometimes this impulsive need to do something would hurt News Corp. and its shareholders. But more often than not, Murdoch's penchant for moving without hesitation has served him and his investors well, as the acquisition of Fox clearly demonstrated.

Still, reaction to the Fox television network announcement within the industry at the time was, to put it mildly, tepid. The *Chicago Sun-Times*, which in October 1985 was still owned by News Corp., noted in a story about the launch that "the idea of a fourth network has seemed such an abstraction in the past that most often when the term is used, media reporters put quotation marks around it, as if to explain that a competitor to

NBC, ABC and CBS would not likely resemble a network in a way viewers understand the concept."[6]

A story in the *Los Angeles Times* suggested that the move came at a curious time, since the percentage of viewers watching the major networks had been shrinking during the past decade.

"Ten years ago, the three major networks, ABC, CBS and NBC, competed for 91 percent of television viewers. That figure is now 77 percent, and dropping. Viewers have abandoned commercial fare for home video and entertainment sources— videocassettes and recorders—or opted for satellite receivers," according to a *Los Angeles Times* story.[7] The report went on to posit that Murdoch stood a great chance of "some success" with the Fox and Metromedia assets in the international market, since his purchase of Fox and the Metromedia stations gave him the international rights to several hit TV shows of the time.

But several analysts were openly skeptical of the network's chances of surviving in, let alone thriving in, the television landscape. "It will take a lot of time for Fox Network to become a success. It is likely to be measured in decades, not years," said Tony Hoffman, an independent media analyst based in New York, in an Associated Press story from October 1985.[8]

The doubts were fueled by the mystery surrounding the network. When Murdoch officially announced the creation of the Fox television network, few people had any idea what types of programs the Fox network planned to run. The only television shows the Fox studio had in production at the time of the launch were all airing on other networks—the *M.A.S.H.* spin-off *Trapper John* was on CBS, as was *Charlie & Co.*, a short-lived sitcom described as CBS' answer to NBC's hit *The Cosby Show*, while the sitcom *Mr. Belvedere* and the Lee Majors action show *The Fall Guy* aired on ABC. The studio claimed it had other shows in development but that many of them were also likely to be shopped to other networks, and not Fox.

"It's going to be a tough road. Fox doesn't currently have any programming of the caliber of a *Dallas* or a *Dynasty*," asserted Merrill Lynch analyst Harold "Hal" Vogel in October 1985, referring to the two highly rated prime-time soaps of the mid-1980s that aired on CBS and ABC, respectively.[9] Vogel now runs his own media investment firm in New York.

But what many in the media world apparently failed to consider was that Murdoch was not going to simply emulate what ABC, CBS and NBC were doing. Instead of being a "me too" network, Fox was often innovative with its programming choices, although many of the shows, just like many of the headlines and stories in his tabloids, offended the sensibilities of more highbrow viewers.

"We at Fox at the moment are deeply involved in working to put shape and form on original programs. These will be shows with no outer limits. The only rules that we will enforce on these programs is they must have taste, they must be engaging, they must be entertaining and they must be original," Murdoch said about Fox in January 1986.[10]

Murdoch, as he did with his newspapers, was once again

demanding that a News Corp. property take bold risks in the name of being "original." Murdoch would not be content launching a new network that simply emulated ABC, CBS and NBC. He, as he often does with new ventures, wanted to create something that his competitors would one day seek to emulate.

By the time the network officially debuted in October 1986, Murdoch had struck agreements with many other independent affiliate local television stations in the United States. So instead of running on just the six Metromedia stations News Corp. had acquired, Fox was immediately available on ninety-six stations, reaching about 80 percent of the nation's overall households. That distribution made Fox a more legitimate challenger to ABC, CBS and NBC rather than being a mere "netlet," as some in the television business derisively referred to Fox.

Still, it did take several years (but not decades) for Fox to emerge as a legitimate alternative to television's "Big Three." The network's first national program, a talk show featuring comedienne Joan Rivers, was a flop. And the network took the calculated risk of slowly launching its prime-time schedule, starting in April 1987 with original shows only on Sunday night. But those shows quickly captured the public's fancy. One was *Married ... with Children*, a raunchy sitcom that turned the character of Al Bundy into a household name as kind of a 1980s version of Archie Bunker. The show aired until 1997 and to this day is still widely credited as putting Fox on the cultural map.

The other show, a self-titled variety program starring British actress and musician Tracey Ullman, was less of a hit, only lasting until 1990. But one of the segments on the show, a crudely animated feature about a dysfunctional family called the Simpsons, turned into a pop culture phenomenon. A half-hour show of *The Simpsons* first aired on Fox in 1989 and it is still running, making it both the longest-airing animated show and longest-running sitcom in television history. The show also spawned a highly successful movie for Fox; *The Simpsons Movie* hit theaters in July 2007 and, according to figures from independent movie industry research firm Box Office Mojo, grossed more than $180 million in the United States and generated global box office sales of more than $525 million.

Thanks to the buzz created by *Married . . . with Children* and *The Simpsons*, Fox launched a slew of other television hits in the 1990s, many of which skewed more toward the viewers that advertisers were lusting after, including sketch comedy show *In Living Color*, a series that launched the careers of Jim Carrey and Jamie Foxx, prime-time soaps *Beverly Hills 90210*, *Melrose Place* and *Party of Five* and sci-fi cult favorite *The X-Files*. By 1993, Fox was airing prime-time shows seven nights a week. But the network was still not yet a true runaway success. That would change after Fox bid for, and won, a lucrative television contract from the National Football League, the king of professional sports in the United States.

Murdoch knew firsthand the importance of sports to a network's viability, having witnessed the role that professional soccer had on the ratings at BSkyB and other networks throughout

Britain and the rest of Europe. To that end, Fox first bid for a small part of the NFL contract in 1987 shortly after the network was launched. It had hoped to win the *Monday Night Football* franchise, which had aired on ABC since its inception in 1970, but the NFL shied away from giving a contract to Fox since the network was still in its infancy. But by 1993, Fox, while still an upstart, was no longer considered as big a risk for the NFL.

Fox bid nearly $1.6 billion for the rights to air games from the NFL's National Football Conference (NFC) for four years—a stunningly rich offer that sparked the usual laments that Murdoch was offering way too much money to get what he wanted. Despite the largesse of the contract, some media observers felt the NFL would prefer to stick with its longtime broadcast partner CBS, which had been airing NFL games since the mid-1950s. But CBS apparently did not approach the level of Fox's offer and the NFL surprised the television and sports world by accepting Fox's bid. Fox began airing NFC football in the fall of 1994 and is still one of the league's key broadcasting partners, having extended its deal with the NFL several times since 1993.

Fox quickly moved to hire most of the on-air personalities from CBS, a signal to loyal football fans that the network was not looking to drastically shake up coverage of their beloved sport. But what really made the NFL deal such a coup for Murdoch and News Corp. was that it allowed him to further increase the distribution of the Fox network. News Corp., primarily on the promise of upcoming NFL coverage, purchased a minority stake in local television station owner New World Communications, which owned many stations affiliated with CBS. In order to make sure that those stations would still be able to air football, many of the New World stations switched from CBS to Fox.

By making this move, Fox accomplished two key goals. The move allowed the network to enter several new markets, but perhaps more importantly the affiliate switch gave Fox access to stations in the more desirable VHF range, channels that were between 2 and 13 on the television dial. The channels on the lower end of the dial were more desirable due to their easy access. Fox, by virtue of the agreements it made with many independent local affiliates when it first launched, aired primarily on lesser-watched UHF channels for the first few years of its existence.

The NFL deal validated Fox and enabled it to eventually bid for and win other lucrative sports broadcasting contracts such as the rights to air Major League Baseball's World Series, college football's Bowl Championship Series, NASCAR's Daytona 500 and other signature NASCAR events. The NFL also gave Fox a platform to promote its shows, which it used to help launch other new hits in the late 1990s such as *Ally McBeal* and *That 70s Show*. But the network hit a rut in the early part of the twenty-first century. With many of its previous hits showing signs of age, Fox changed tactics and got an early start on the reality television craze that currently dominates television today. Many of the shows that Fox debuted, though, were beyond the lowest common denominator. The titles of the programs, let alone the actual content, were ripe for derision and mockery: *When Animals Attack, Who Wants to Marry a Multi-Millionaire* and *Temptation Island*, to name a few.

Was the company that had its roots in the legendary 20th Century Fox studio doomed to a slow, painful descent into cultural oblivion now that the twentieth century was over? That, needless to say, was not to be the case. In 2000, News Corp. added even more affiliates to the Fox network through the acquisition of television station owner Chris-Craft Industries. And thanks in large part to a singing contest imported from Britain called *American Idol*, which first aired on Fox in 2002, the network enjoyed not just a renaissance but started to post its highest ratings ever.

In addition to *Idol* and the strong ratings generated by the network's continued NFL coverage, Fox also launched several other new hits in the mid-2000s, including the medical procedural drama *House* and the action thriller *24*. In February 2004, Fox won its first so-called sweeps month, a key period used by networks and marketers to establish advertising rates for the upcoming season. The network went on to win the ratings battle for the 18- to 49-year-old demographic for the entire 2004–2005 season and did so again the next two seasons.

Fox also won the ratings race in 2007–2008. In fact, through early March 2008, Fox was the only network to see a boost in viewers for the 2007–2008 television season. This was a significant feat considering that many television viewers fled prime-time network television in droves as a result of the Writers Guild of America strike that lasted from late 2007 to early 2008, a work stoppage that caused most networks to run out of original television programming on many big hits by November 2007.

This is not to say that Fox was free of any missteps during its rise to the top of the television rankings. At the same time Fox was enjoying its biggest successes, News Corp. decided to launch another national network called MyNetworkTV, with the hopes of turning that into another Fox. The jury is still out on whether MyNetworkTV, which was launched seemingly on a whim as a quick response to a move by competitors, will ever be more than a perennial money-loser for Fox and News Corp.

In February 2006, News Corp. boldly proclaimed that it was launching MyNetworkTV, a channel that would feature in prime time English-language telenovelas, soap operas modeled after Spanish-language television shows that are popular around the globe. But MyNetworkTV was not something that had been in careful development for years. It was simply a means for Murdoch to have some prime-time programming for a handful of his local television stations not affiliated with Fox, which were about to face a rude awakening.

Several News Corp.–owned stations were affiliated with another network called UPN. And that network was about to be replaced by another new network. This would leave the former UPN affiliates with a huge programming void.

On the heels of Fox's success in the mid-1990s, CBS and

Time Warner both launched their own youth-oriented networks. CBS' was called UPN, while Time Warner's was known as the WB. While each network had some individual hits, they both struggled and neither was considered a legitimate number five to the Big Four of television, which now included Fox. So in a move that stunned many in the television industry, CBS and Time Warner decided to merge UPN and the WB and created a new network, known as the CW, which would launch in September 2006 with some programs from UPN and some from the WB.

This was a problem for Murdoch, since News Corp. owned ten television stations that were affiliated with UPN—and these stations were not going to be the ones carrying the new CW when it launched. "Nature and TV abhor a vacuum and one was quickly created with the merger that spawned the CW," said John Rash, senior vice president and director of broadcast negotiations with Campbell Mithun, a Minneapolis-based media-buying firm, at the time of the MyNetworkTV announcement.[11]

The decision to hastily cobble together plans for a new network was in many ways classic Murdoch. But without having a concrete plan in place to attract viewers, the network faced an uphill battle, despite having what Rash said was a big benefit due to the fact that "the people behind this [MyNetworkTV] have been remarkably successful in nearly every genre of TV." To Fox's credit, it was able to convince many other affiliate station owners that they should sign on to MyNetworkTV since they would be left out in the cold following the CW's launch. By the time MyNetworkTV launched, it had deals to air on stations covering 96 percent of all available households in the country. So distribution would not be a problem.

But Murdoch and Fox seriously miscalculated Americans' interest in serialized nighttime soaps. The hook of MyNetworkTV and challenge for viewers was that each program would air five nights a week and the story would wrap up within thirteen-week cycles. That demanded a lot of the viewers' time and attention. American viewers were used to catching their favorite shows once—or in the case of reality hits like *American Idol* maybe twice—a week. So what played well in Mexico and South America did not fare well in the ratings within the United States. And it didn't help that the casts of the first two telenovelas, *Desire* and *Fashion House*, featured largely unknown actors and actresses.

The network's name was also an issue. What did MyNetworkTV mean? Was it an attempt to latch on to the success of MySpace? Individual stations referred to themselves as My followed by their channel number; for example, News Corp.–owned WWOR in New York, which aired on Channel 9, was rebranded "My9."

The telenovelas subsequently debuted with anemic ratings, and by early 2007 the network's new president announced MyNetworkTV would scale back the telenovelas to only two nights a week and would broadcast more reality and extreme sports programming. That did not do much for ratings either.

By the fall of 2007, MyNetworkTV completely abandoned the telenovela format and added shows with names that sounded like rejects from Fox when that network hit its reality nadir a few years earlier, such as *Celebrity Exposé* and *Whacked Out Videos*.

Peter Chernin admitted during News Corp.'s earnings conference call in February 2007 that MyNetworkTV was a major source of angst for Fox but expressed hope that the network's fortunes would turn around. "MyNetworkTV is not going as we originally planned. There will always be fits and starts when you undertake the launch of any network," Chernin said. "But we will roll out new program changes in MyNetworkTV in the months ahead to lower costs and hopefully lead to higher ratings. Clearly, we've made mistakes but I'm confident the worst is behind us. We'll have better, cheaper and more advertiser friendly programming going forward."

But a year after those remarks, MyNetworkTV was still a work in progress. Despite the heavy emphasis on reality television programming, the network did not meaningfully benefit from the writers' strike. However, News Corp. chief financial officer Dave DeVoe said during News Corp.'s earnings conference call in February 2008 that he was heartened by the fact that MyNetworkTV reported lower losses. And the network was still experimenting with programming. It embraced the sitcom format with a program starring rapper-turned-reality-show-star Flavor Flav in the spring of 2008 and signed a deal to start broadcasting World Wrestling Entertainment's *WWE*

SmackDown! show, formerly of the CW, beginning in the fall of 2008.

If MyNetworkTV is eventually scrapped, which is not out of the realm of possibility, it would represent that rarest of instances in Murdoch's career, a complete strategic misstep. It wouldn't be the first, though. In fact, one of News Corp.'s other notable strategic blunders involved Fox. In a move that eventually backfired, Murdoch, under pressure from shareholders to boost News Corp.'s overall stock price in the late 1990s, made the mistake of selling off a 20 percent stake in Fox to the public as a separately traded stock called Fox Entertainment Group. In theory, separating Fox from News Corp.'s stodgier assets—newspapers and HarperCollins—was meant to highlight the sexier growth prospects in the Fox television and movie studio as well as the fledgling cable networks birthed in the mid-1990s.

But shares of Fox actually wound up underperforming News Corp.'s stock for large stretches of time after the spin-off. And while some thought the separation creating another stock for Fox would make News Corp. an easier company to understand and value, the converse wound up being true. By 2005, News Corp. had tired of having the separate stock listing and the company announced in January that it was offering to buy back the remaining stake in Fox that it did not already own. The original offer was deemed too low by some Fox shareholders, however, forcing News Corp. to increase the amount of News

Corp. shares it was offering in exchange for Fox in March 2005. The sweetened deal allowed News Corp. to complete the purchase of all outstanding Fox shares later that month. Murdoch, in his annual speech to shareholders in October 2005, argued that the decision was made to bring Fox completely back into the News Corp. fold because it would end up "simplifying our corporate structure and giving us full access to the growing earnings of the Fox operations."[12]

The poor reception to the Fox spin-off is apparently not something that Murdoch has forgotten. In the past few years, since the company has boosted its presence in the online media segment through a series of acquisitions, some analysts have asked Murdoch if he would one day consider spinning off a portion of Fox Interactive Media, the News Corp. unit that owns the rapidly growing MySpace social network, in order to realize greater value for the division from the market. The argument from these analysts, which sounds suspiciously familiar to the calls to spin off Fox years earlier, is that MySpace and other FIM assets would fetch a higher multiple from investors if it were freed up from the constraints of slower-growth News Corp. business such as newspapers and book publishing.

And while Wall Street analysts may have incredibly short memories, Murdoch does not. He is resisting the clarion call to spin off MySpace precisely because of the Fox fiasco. Speaking at a Goldman Sachs media conference in September 2006, Murdoch dismissed the idea of a spin-off of the Fox Interactive

Media unit or of any other divisions, for that matter. "We tried that with Fox and it didn't work," he said.[13]

So Murdoch clearly remembers his mistakes. But he also remembers his successes and is not shy about reminding his rivals about them. Murdoch has boasted numerous times throughout the years about how News Corp. defied the odds and went against the grain when deciding to create Fox. He seems to derive great satisfaction, if not outright glee, in reminding his critics how wrong they were.

During testimony to the U.S. House Committee on the Judiciary at a 2003 hearing about News Corp.'s proposal to buy a stake in U.S. satellite television company DirecTV, Murdoch frequently touted how not only was Fox a commercial success for his company, but a benefit to American television viewers.

"Our company has a history of challenging the established— and often stagnant—media with new products and services for television viewers around the world. Perhaps our first and best-known effort to offer new choices to consumers in the broadcasting arena came with the establishment of the Fox network in 1986. Fox brought much-needed competition to the 'Big 3' broadcast networks at a time when conventional wisdom said it couldn't be done," Murdoch said.[14]

Two years later, in his speech to the American Society of Newspaper Editors, Murdoch was at it again, crowing once more about how Fox had changed the television industry.

"At News Corporation, we have a history of challenging

media orthodoxies. Nearly twenty years ago, we created a fourth broadcast network. What was behind that creation was a fundamental questioning of the way people got their nightly entertainment to that point. We weren't constrained by the news at six, primetime at eight, news again at 11 paradigm. We weren't constrained by the belief that entertainment had to be geared to a particular audience, or reflect a certain mind-set. Instead, we shortened the primetime block to two hours, pushed up the news by an hour, and programmed the network to a younger-skewing audience. The result was the Fox Broadcast Network, today America's number one network among 18- to 49-year-olds," Murdoch said in April 2005.[15]

So competitors and others in the industry may have underestimated Murdoch's almost compulsive need to show his critics time and time again that they are wrong. And more than anything else, the success of Fox also highlighted a side of Murdoch that many rivals probably were not aware of, the side that doesn't mind letting someone else take the lead.

Murdoch trusted Barry Diller, who was widely acknowledged as one of the more creative programming minds in the industry, to come up with a plan to make Fox into something unique. Murdoch would delegate in a similar fashion with Peter Chernin—having him lead the television operations and later the movie studio. Chernin is now Murdoch's second-in-command. Murdoch's willingess to relegate was also the case with Roger Ailes, whom Murdoch lured away from CNBC in 1996 to start the Fox News Channel. And Murdoch would also act in a relatively hands-off manner with the social networking site MySpace, allowing the site's cofounder Chris DeWolfe to continue to head the site and play an active role in the site's strategic moves.

Murdoch does not get enough credit for his willingness to step aside and let others take charge when he is not the voice of authority. This certainly does not mean that Murdoch sits passively by or that he isn't the final arbiter when it comes to decisions regarding Fox, cable channels and the Web. But he appears to realize that the only way to successfully build a business is to loosen the reins and not be an all-controlling micromanager.

Scores of Murdoch's newspaper editors past and present would probably disagree with this characterization of Murdoch, and they would not be wrong. But there is a marked difference in how Murdoch interacts with managers in businesses outside of his comfort zone, that is, outside of the newspaper business. The demonization of Murdoch in the mainstream press can be extreme, with much of the negative coverage due to envy of his fortune and power, disdain for his political beliefs or, in many cases, a potent combination of both. But it is clear that News Corp. would not and could not be as successful as it is if Murdoch ruled the empire with absolute autocratic power. At some point, he learned to listen to advisers and realized that others possessed strengths that he may have lacked. And that seemed to start with Diller and Fox.

The fact that Murdoch and Diller coexisted as long as they did is a sign that Murdoch can tolerate other headstrong executives in his organization, provided they deliver strong results for the company.

"He's hard on people who do not perform to the standards he feels are necessary," says Richard Dorfman of investment firm Richard Alan. "But once he has his people in place, he doesn't just willy-nilly change horses. I don't think it is fair to say he's a difficult guy to work for."[16]

Still, many media observers openly wondered if Murdoch would even hang on to Diller after he bought Fox in 1985. But Diller, who prior to joining Fox was the head of Paramount Pictures, then owned by Gulf & Western, and was widely credited for overseeing the development of several big hits at that studio in the 1980s, including *Raiders of the Lost Ark*, *Ordinary People*, *48 Hours*, *Flashdance*, *Terms of Endearment* and *Beverly Hills Cop*. Diller clearly had the Hollywood savvy and experience that Murdoch— who up until that point in his career was still known mainly as a publishing mogul—lacked.

Diller finally left Fox in 1992 to buy a stake in home shopping network QVC, an investment that would lay the foundation for Diller's own media empire, the sprawling online conglomerate IAC. In an interview with the British newspaper the *Guardian* in 2006, Diller said that he had a great working relationship with Murdoch, despite Murdoch's reputation as a meddlesome executive. He joked that he wasn't sure how much longer he could have stayed at Fox without eventually butting heads with Murdoch, but that during his tenure there the two men had only two disagreements, which he would not elaborate on.

"He is one of the greatest risk-taking people I have ever known. There would have been a row if I'd stayed, but we had a fantastic eight years," Diller said.[7]

The fact that Diller cites Murdoch's risk-taking as a compliment and sign of respect is not a surprise, considering that he has taken many of his own risks in building up IAC, most of which have not panned out as well as Murdoch's businesses. And it is somewhat ironic that Diller had to fight for control of IAC with media investor John Malone, who almost wound up gaining control of News Corp. in the late 1990s following a struggle with Murdoch. But the comment is a perfect illustration of Murdoch's nature. He never seems to be satisfied with playing it safe. And with the Fox broadcast network no longer being derisively referred to as "the fourth network" by the mid-1990s, it was time for Murdoch to take his next big risk. Murdoch was about to venture into the even more fragmented world of cable television, and in the process attempt to prove to an unbelieving industry that there was room in television for more than one twenty-four-hour news network. He had already humbled ABC, CBS and NBC. Now it was time for Murdoch to try and do the same to CNN and its enigmatic owner, Ted Turner. Murdoch and Turner butt heads frequently because of their political differences. But some would argue that the two do not get along simply because their personalities are so similar.

CHAPTER 3

Hooked on Cable

In 1996, Murdoch embarked on his next challenge: convincing the media world that not only was there room for another twenty-four-hour cable news channel besides CNN, but that there was a need for it. Bill Clinton would soon be elected to a second term as president in November of that year and Murdoch noticed a growing dissatisfaction among conservatives. He thought they could be better served by having a network that aired more of their viewpoints. After all, many radio shows featuring conservative hosts fared quite well in the ratings.

The perception was that CNN had a left-leaning bias, a notion that was perpetuated due to the fact that Turner, CNN's founder, was unabashedly liberal. Murdoch would create his new channel under the guise of giving a more "fair and balanced" presentation of the news, in which on-air personalities would merely "report" and let the viewers "decide." He recruited

Roger Ailes from GE's NBC Universal in 1996 to help him start the Fox News Channel. Before becoming a television executive, Ailes was a political consultant for Republican presidents Ronald Reagan and George H. W. Bush as well as for New York City mayor Rudolph Giuliani.

Once again, Murdoch was planning to defy conventional wisdom. And just as with the Fox broadcast network, Fox News would eventually turn out to be another huge success for News Corp.

"We sensed ten years ago that people watching television news felt alienated by the monolithic presentation of the news they were getting from the nightly news broadcasts or cable networks. We sensed that there was another way we could deliver that news—objectively, fairly, and faster-paced. And the result was the Fox News Channel, today America's number one cable news network," Murdoch said in his speech to the American Society of Newspaper Editors in April 2005.[1]

The importance of Fox News and other cable networks to News Corp. cannot be understated. In the past few decades, viewers have increasingly tuned out the big broadcasters, and cable networks have been the beneficiary of this trend. While advertising spending growth on broadcast networks has been sluggish for the past few years, advertising sales growth on cable networks has continued to be fairly robust. In the first nine months of 2007, according to figures from research firm TNS Media Intelligence, cable advertising sales rose 4.7 percent from the same period in 2006, while network television ad revenue dipped 3 percent and national syndication ad sales fell 4.6 percent. And for 2008, TNS predicted that cable television advertising revenue would be up 5 percent compared to just 2.7 percent growth for network television and 1.3 percent for syndicated television.

Cable network owners rely on more than just advertising dollars, though. They also receive payments, known as carriage fees, from cable companies, phone companies and satellite television operators for the right to include the channels in their offerings to customers. And when a cable network enjoys healthy ratings, the network owners often have the upper hand in gaining higher carriage fees from the distributors, which Fox News would use to its full benefit when it was negotiating new carriage contracts with the big cable providers in 2006 and 2007. Cable, simply put, is a better business model than broadcast television.

It is for this reason that virtually all the major media conglomerates in the United States, and not just News Corp., have been boosting their presence in cable. Time Warner, in addition to CNN, owns the successful networks TNT, Turner Broadcasting System and Cartoon Network. Viacom owns MTV, Nickelodeon, BET, Spike and Comedy Central. Disney has arguably the crown jewel of cable networks in ESPN and also owns the Disney Channel and ABC Family, which it acquired from News Corp. when it was known as Fox Family in 1996. NBC Universal, the media arm of General Electric whose NBC network has struggled for the past few years, owns USA, Bravo, SCI FI and

CNBC, and acquired the women's cable network Oxygen in 2007 and the Weather Channel in 2008. All these networks have been bright spots for NBC Universal.

Once Murdoch got a taste of how lucrative the cable market could be with Fox News, he quickly sought to capitalize on that success and the strong brand name of Fox and launched several other channels. News Corp. owns a network of regional sports channels in top markets such as Atlanta, Dallas and Los Angeles, dubbed Fox Sports Net. The company also owns FX, a channel that has made a name for itself with edgy programs that have also been critical darlings, such as *The Shield*, *Rescue Me*, *Nip/Tuck*, and *Damages*.

And cable, while not the largest business segment of News Corp., is perhaps the most important, as it has the potential to soon become the biggest contributor to sales and profits for the entire company. In the first nine months of News Corp.'s fiscal 2008, the cable segment was, by far, the most rapidly growing unit of the company's major business segments. Sales from the cable networks rose 29 percent in the first three quarters of the fiscal year. Operating profits surged nearly 20 percent, trailing only the 47 percent growth in operating profits from Fox's broadcast television business and a threefold increase in profits at News Corp.'s satellite television division. The cable segment's operating margins of 26.5 percent are the highest of all of News Corp.'s businesses.

What makes the cable division's performance even more impressive is that it came at a time when News Corp. was spending heavily to launch two new networks in the fall of 2007: if News Corp. wasn't spending so heavily to launch Fox Business Network and the Big Ten Network, profits might have been even higher. The latter network is a channel devoted to sports programming tied to the colleges and universities in the Big Ten Conference, which includes some of the largest schools in the nation (and thousands of loyal and wealthy alumni), such as the University of Michigan, Ohio State University and Penn State University. The Big Ten owns the majority of the channel, while News Corp. owns a minority stake.

But it is Fox News that drives the majority of the cable network divison's growth. While News Corp. does not specifically break down how much revenue and profits the channel generates, the company did say that in its first three quarters of fiscal 2008, Fox News' sales rose 24 percent compared to 9 percent growth in sales at the company's FX entertainment channel and 9 percent at its regional sports networks. News Corp. attributed the strong results at Fox News to higher revenues from affiliates carrying the channel on their cable systems. That's because the channel had more subscribers, which meant the affiliates paid higher fees to carry Fox News.

The company also said the network generated higher advertising rates thanks to increased ratings. News Corp. boasted that Fox News' viewership in prime time was more than 40 percent greater than CNN's during the fiscal third quarter and that ratings on a twenty-four-hour basis were also more than 40 percent higher than CNN's.

Few could have predicted in 1996 that Fox would one day supplant CNN. Even Murdoch was more cautious than usual. During a press conference in late January of that year to announce the hiring of Ailes and the launch of Fox News, Murdoch admitted that going toe-to-toe with CNN and the news operations of the major networks would not be easy. The Fox broadcast network, after all, relied on its local affiliates to provide news for the Fox network as opposed to having a substantial, dedicated national news division.

"We have a lot of work ahead of us," Murdoch said during the press conference, adding that he expected ABC, NBC and CBS, going forward, would continue to spend more on their news operations than Fox.[2] He estimated that News Corp. would initially spend about $50 million annually on Fox News, in addition to the $30 million or so that the company was spending before the channel's launch. By way of comparison, the major networks were each spending in the range of hundreds of millions of dollars.

Murdoch did not seem daunted by the financial disadvantage Fox News would face. It's intriguing that a man who has a reputation for overspending on acquisitions and programming throughout his career dismissed the notion that money mattered when it came to news. "Dollars don't equate to quality. That's not our model," he said.[3]

But Murdoch was realistic enough to realize that getting the channel onto cable systems would prove to be more difficult than launching the Fox broadcast network. Convincing independent local station owners desperate for any original content to compete against ABC, CBS and NBC in 1986 to affiliate with Fox was one thing. Convincing big cable system owners that they should carry Fox News when they already had CNN, and in some cases America's Talking—a new channel from NBC that would eventually change its name to MSNBC—was another issue entirely. So Murdoch would not make any bold proclamations about how many subscribers he thought Fox News would have at its launch, saying at a press conference that any number "would only be a guess."

Not surprisingly, at the outset many media observers downplayed Fox News' chances of success. Murdoch would have been surprised if pundits had responded differently. A story published in the *New York Times* about the launch of Fox News and hiring of Ailes suggested that the creation of the Fox News Channel "was to give Mr. Ailes a toy to play with, though, given the current state of Fox News as described by some insiders, it may be less a toy than an imaginary friend."[4]

The article went on to quote one former Fox executive as saying, "There is no there, there," about Fox's news efforts, as well as a current staff member of Fox News saying that "the thing to notice about Fox News is that they keep announcing things that never happen."[5]

A story in Turner's and CNN's hometown newspaper the *Atlanta Journal-Constitution* cited a "confidential study" commissioned by a leading cable provider which "found that cable subscribers were satisfied with CNN and were little interested in more news channels."[6]

One media buyer posited that there may not be enough advertising dollars to support more than one twenty-four-hour news network and suggested that with America's Talking changing to MSNBC, there was simply too much competition.

"It's a fascinating horse race and someone must think advertisers have lots of dollars, pound notes or lira and want to reach a news audience," said Betsy Frank, executive vice president and director of strategic media resources at Zenith Media Services, to trade publication *Electronic Media* in February 1996. "Even if they appeal to different people than the CNN audience, one has to wonder whether they are slicing the pie and making the pieces smaller. There may be some disappointments."[7]

CBS News president Andrew Heyward said in the same article that there should be "healthy skepticism" of the new cable news networks and added that they "smack slightly of vaporware."[8]

Fox News officially debuted in October with a mix of news and opinion that is still the hallmark of the network's approach today. To say the least, many of the critical reviews were quite savage.

"CNN was born in 1980 amid concern in some circles that Ted Turner, then a maverick conservative, would use his pioneering twenty-four-hour-a-day news network to boost his political views. A similar buzz greeted Monday's arrival of right-wing media baron Rupert Murdoch's round-the-clock Fox News Channel (FNC). One difference: Turner isn't doing it, Murdoch is," wrote Howard Rosenberg in the *Los Angeles Times.*[9]

Rosenberg went on to add that maybe the "new network was just having one of those rare biased days"—one that Murdoch and Ailes "accuse mainstream media of having all the time on behalf of Democrats and liberals." He suggested that Murdoch and Ailes "are, in their mind, merely evening the score."[10]

He further dubbed the network's "More News in Less Time" slogan as "a euphemism for shallowness," and noted that many of the channel's "uneven, youngish, relatively green editorial staffers … look as if they've gotten off at the wrong bus stop."[11]

Washington Post media critic Howard Kurtz had the following to say about the network's first day on the air: "Fox's daytime news is nothing revolutionary. The Ken-and-Barbie anchor teams do a credible job of cruising through the headlines, but there's no more depth than you'd see on your typical Action News."[12]

Manuel Mendoza of the *Dallas Morning News* declared that "in lieu of facts, Fox often relied on polls, pundits and British-style tabloid journalism during its first day on the air, contradicting the 'fair and balanced' approach that Fox News chairman and CEO Roger Ailes promised. Fox reported and decided." And media reporters from the *Wall Street Journal* wrote that Fox "tried a few new tricks to distinguish itself from archrival Cable

News Network, but they were mostly cosmetic. The channel labels live reports 'now,' and some analysis of the presidential debates was labeled 'spin,' to reflect the partisan biases of the analysts."[13]

There were also unflattering critiques of the nighttime lineup of personality-driven talk shows. The *Oregonian* newspaper of Portland pointed out that Bill O'Reilly was "brash, irreverent and often obnoxious" and that his interview with then-President Clinton's drug czar Barry McCaffrey "seemed to feature more of O'Reilly's long-winded and opinionated questioning rather than McCaffrey's answers."[14] And Kurtz lamented that on the *Hannity & Colmes* show "their combined decibel level drowns out the guests, who respond by trying to out-bellow the hosts."[15]

Several media critics also complained about the visual graphics on the network, with Kurtz pointing out that "brief snippets and factoids keep popping up onto the screen ('Dole is a member of the Shriners and the Elks') while they are talking, which can be EXTREMELY ANNOYING when you're trying to listen."[16]

Fox News has succeeded in spite of the critics' barbs. Not only that, it seems that Fox News is a success because of what the critics complained most about. The "snippets and factoids" that Kurtz found so bothersome would eventually be copied by all other news outlets, particularly CNN.

For better or worse, it's impossible to turn on any newscast and not be bombarded with a dizzying array of streaming text that competes with, and does often distract from, the other images on the screen. And the opinionated talk shows that Fox ran in prime time in lieu of news reports not only remain the model for Fox News but also now for CNN, its sister network Headline News and MSNBC as well. In other words, Murdoch did it again. He not only succeeded in supplanting his rivals, he forced them to adapt to what he was doing in order for them to remain competitive with him.

And despite the many doubts of media veterans that Fox News could supplant CNN, with its sixteen-year head start and unofficial title of king of cable news, it seemed that Turner felt that Fox News posed a legitimate threat, even from the channel's earliest days. Turner took many potshots at Murdoch and his conservative viewpoints; he seemed to take Murdoch's launch of Fox News as a personal affront. Most notably, Turner launched a blistering attack against Murdoch, calling him out on what Turner believed were Murdoch's ambitions to dominate the global news landscape in a November 1996 speech at, of all places, the United Nations.

"Already you can see that there is a new group coming, led by that no-good SOB Rupert Murdoch. They want to control the world. They want to control the television world. We have got to do everything we can to stop them," Ted Turner said. He continued that Murdoch "wants to sit here and control Indian television in India; he wants to control Chinese television in China. Bullshit!" When asked what could be done, Turner replied, "This is a battle between good and evil," before concluding that "I don't want to talk about that no-good bastard anymore."[17]

Keep in mind that this was merely one month after Fox News was launched. At the time, the network was hardly the ratings juggernaut it is now. In fact, Fox News was facing a tough battle to get cable systems to even distribute the channel in the first place. When Fox News debuted on October 7, 1996, it was only available in about 17 million cable households, a far cry from the 66 million households that CNN was in at the time. Fox News was not yet available to cable subscribers in either New York or Los Angeles, the country's two largest television markets. Time Warner, which owned CNN, also owned most of the cable systems in New York.

This aggravated Murdoch to no end. News Corp. even went to court to get Time Warner to carry the channel. News Corp. claimed Time Warner originally agreed to carry the channel in New York but backed out after Time Warner completed its acquisition of Turner Broadcasting System in the summer of 1996. Giuliani, who was mayor of New York City at the time, publicly supported News Corp., claiming that Fox might leave New York, resulting in job losses, if the network was not given a spot on Time Warner's cable systems.

So in many respects the battle between Fox News and CNN was personal and more than just a fight between two large corporations. It was also a war between two outsized egos. Turner's distaste for Murdoch was arguably matched by Murdoch's loathing of Turner. And Murdoch took particular glee in ribbing Turner at every turn.

During a World Series game in October 1996, while the Atlanta Braves, which Turner bought in 1976 and which also became part of Time Warner once Time Warner acquired Turner Broadcasting System, were playing the New York Yankees at Yankee Stadium, a plane flew over the stadium and repeatedly flashed the following message: "Hey Ted. Be Brave. Don't Censor the Fox News Channel."[18]

The plane had been hired by Fox and was probably the politest of attacks between Murdoch and Turner. Ever since News Corp. announced its plans to launch Fox News, Murdoch and Turner traded nasty barbs. Turner mainly used his razor-sharp tongue to specifically attack Murdoch, while Murdoch, more often than not, let his news outlets do the talking for him. Not that he was completely silent when it came to the topic of Turner. Shortly after announcing plans for Fox News, Murdoch accused Turner, in a speech delivered at the National Press Club in Washington in February 1996, of having "sold out to the establishment in his declining years" and "brown-nosing foreign dictators."[19]

But it was through Fox and the *New York Post* that Murdoch let his ire for Turner really be known. Fox, which was airing the World Series games in 1996, made it a point to only show Turner when he looked his most foolish, such as while wearing

a Braves hat sideways and doing the team's trademark toma-
hawk chop arm motion, which, incidentally, many Native
Americans found offensive. Earlier in 1996, the *New York Post*
published an article about Turner's then-wife, actress and political activist Jane Fonda, that referred to her as "just another
scatty-brained Hollywood nude-nik" and included a photo of
her sitting on top of a North Vietnamese cannon during her
controversial visit to Hanoi in 1972.[20] That story was published
shortly after Fonda questioned if Giuliani's support for News
Corp. had something to do with the fact that his then-wife
Donna Hanover Giuliani was a reporter for the News Corp.–
owned television station WNYW in New York.

The *Post* also poked fun at Turner's admitted battle against
depression, wondering in a 1996 article if he "had come off the
medication?" and if he was "veering dangerously toward insan-
ity?"[21] Turner, meanwhile, resorted to name-calling throughout
1996, referring to Murdoch as a "scumbag," a "disgrace to journalism" and "slime" on various occasions. Turner even went
as far as to compare Murdoch to Hitler in the way that Murdoch used his news organizations to advance his political interests, saying that he was like the "late Führer."[22] That remark
did not help Turner look sympathetic in his fight against Murdoch. Turner subsequently wound up apologizing to the Anti-
Defamation League as a result. In a letter to the Anti-Defamation
League, Turner wrote that his characterization of Murdoch was
meant to refer "only to the way Hitler managed the news in

Germany" and "was not intended to offend nor to trivialize the role of an individual who wreaked so much havoc upon the Jewish people."[23]

Rivals of both Murdoch and Turner found the battle amusing, to say the least. John Malone, who at the time was the owner of TCI, the nation's second-largest cable company (it would later be sold to AT&T and then Comcast), told British newspaper the *Independent* in November 1996 that watching Murdoch and Turner trade punches was better than a Mike Tyson fight. Malone was an investor in Time Warner when he said this—it would be two and half years before Malone would amass his first stake in News Corp.—but he also had a stake in Murdoch's success, since TCI, unlike Time Warner, had agreed to carry Fox News.

"This is great comedy to me. Ted Turner hasn't felt so young and energetic in years. He loves a good fight. I would waste no tears over either of these guys," Malone said.[24]

And Turner would not let it go. He even picked up on Malone's boxing analogy. In two separate speeches in June 1997, Turner joked about fighting Murdoch. At a Hollywood Radio & Television Society event, he asked attendees the following question about his feud with Murdoch.

"What would you say about he and I going into the ring and putting on the gloves at the MGM Grand in Vegas for a pay-per-view event for charity? We'd charge $4.95 and the winner would get to pick which charity. Nobody has seen two sixty-year-olds fight in a long time. The regular boxers fight at forty.

He's tough. He might beat me. The reason I haven't done this before is that he's seven years older than me, and I'm afraid he'd beat me," Turner said.[25] He brought up the possibility of a bout again at a national convention of sports editors later in the month, quipping that it could be touted as "*Rocky* for Old Guys" and declaring that "Murdoch is probably chicken. If he wants, he can wear headgear and I won't."[26]

Murdoch and Turner finally entered into a period of détente when Time Warner agreed to carry Fox News in July 1997 and the two companies settled their legal differences resulting from the dispute. But the two men would remain fierce foes. In November 1999, for example, Murdoch suggested during an interview on Fox News that he heard Turner, still a vice chairman at Time Warner, was urging Time Warner to make a bid to buy NBC from General Electric.[27] Murdoch didn't cite any sources for this speculation and many openly wondered if his comments were nothing more than a way to possibly put a dent in Time Warner's stock price and further get under Turner's skin.

Murdoch would ultimately find that the greatest way to irritate Turner (and others in the news business) was simply to keep doing what he had been doing with Fox all along: spin that the network was the one "objective" news outlet amid the bastion of liberal news organizations. Slowly but surely the approach worked, and as Fox began to get picked up by more and more cable systems, more viewers embraced Fox's opinionated take on the news. Murdoch also spent heavily on the channel to ensure that it would take off. During his annual comments to shareholders in October 2007, Murdoch said that News Corp. had invested around $900 million in Fox News since its launch.[28] Both Ailes and Murdoch have acknowledged on several occasions that Fox News lost money during its first five years.

But the network was able to reach its goal of surpassing CNN's ratings in just four years, a year ahead of schedule, and the network built on those gains in the years to come. The success of Fox News helped News Corp. when it was launching other new networks, such as FX and the regional sports channels, since cable companies were eager to stay on Murdoch's good side. To that end, the Fox Business Channel, which has had a tepid start, launched on more than 30 million households, the largest-ever debut for a new cable channel.

In fact, Murdoch was so confident about momentum continuing for Fox News and FX that he publicly began calling for higher carriage fees from cable outlets as early as 2004—two years before most of the old Fox News agreements were set to expire.

"When the channel's affiliation agreements begin to expire in 2006, we expect to negotiate carriage rates that match Fox News's exceptional audience numbers. Similarly, our general entertainment channel, FX, is in line for higher affiliate revenues as its original agreements come up for renegotiation in the coming years," Murdoch said in his annual address to shareholders in October 2004.[29]

And once more, just as Murdoch was able to completely

trust Barry Diller when News Corp. first launched the Fox broadcast network in 1986, Murdoch had, in Ailes, a veteran that he knew he could count on fully.

"Ailes is different from all the other people who have gone to work for Murdoch," wrote media columnist Marvin Kitman of *Newsday* shortly after Murdoch hired him in February 1996. "Roger doesn't need the job, being a noted political consultant and president maker (Bush, Nixon), TV producer (*The Rush Limbaugh Show*) and talk-show host (CNBC's *Straightforward*). This time Murdoch has hired somebody who is as big a deal as he is. Ailes can pick up the phone and get the president of the United States, in either party, a lot faster than Rupert can."[30]

And Murdoch has rewarded Ailes handsomely for the success of Fox News, which as of the end of 2007 was available in 95 million households. In 2005, Murdoch named Ailes the chairman of Fox Television Stations, giving Ailes control over the Twentieth Television unit that produces first-run syndicated programming and distributes off-network programming. Ailes was also put in charge as chairman and CEO of Fox Business upon that network's launch.

According to the company's proxy statement for fiscal 2007, which ended in June of that year, Ailes' total annual compensation, including salary, bonuses and other perks, was nearly $11 million.

But because of Murdoch's loyalty to Ailes, Fox News, like nearly every other news organization owned by Murdoch, continues to face criticism about what is perceived to be a conservative bias. In fact, some would argue that Fox News is the worst example of Murdoch using the airwaves to get what he wants politically or financially.

Ailes and Murdoch have repeatedly denied these claims, however. In a meeting with communications committee members of Britain's House of Lords looking into media ownership in the United Kingdom in September 2007, Ailes declared that no such bias exists. According to minutes from the meeting, Ailes "stated that the channel has no particular political agenda and an effort is made to balance the stories they produce" but also conceded that "on some days the channel acts as a balance to the rest of the media," adding that he believed other news outlets, such as the *New York Times*, do have a liberal bias.[31]

Ailes also told the committee members that Fox News never endorses a specific political party or candidate and that the network has had its fair share of stories that did not portray the Republican Party or President George W. Bush in a favorable light. He informed the committee that during the 2000 presidential election, Fox News decided to run a story about Bush being caught driving under the influence of alcohol in 1984 because the network thought it was newsworthy. Ailes said the Bush campaign even asked the network to hold the story. Ailes suggested that the "under the influence" story was the reason Bush lost so much ground to Gore in the final days of the campaign, leading to the closest presidential election in American history. Ailes reiterated that he thought the network had a more centrist view and stated, according to the minutes, that "if any other news channel were to move away from the left then Fox would have stiff competition."[32]

But Murdoch, in his own meeting with House of Lords communication committee members in September 2007, specifically avoided mentioning anything about political bias when describing the reasons he thought Fox News was so successful. According to the minutes of this meeting, he expressed frustration that BSkyB's Sky News was not more like Fox News and that it did not necessarily have to adopt similar editorial views as Fox News in order to become "a proper alternative to the BBC." He argued that the network could make some changes in the way it visually presented the news and employ some of the techniques that had worked so well for Fox News. He concluded that the only reason that Sky News was not more like Fox News was that "nobody at Sky listens to me."[33]

That is probably not entirely true. Clearly, newspaper editors and television news executives have made it a point to listen to Murdoch, or at the very least do things the way they think he would want them done in order to avoid hearing complaints from their bosses, or even Murdoch himself. And Murdoch's fierce sense of ambition will not let Sky News continue to simply plod along; at some point, he will make his voice heard and someone at Sky will listen to him.

Murdoch has grand plans for his cable operations. During his address to shareholders in October 2007, he boldly predicted that Fox News would report a profit of at least $900 million a year within the next few years. He also said the value of the channel would hit the $10 billion mark.[34]

Murdoch is also banking on Fox Business replicating the ratings and financial achievements of Fox News, albeit on a lesser scale. However, Murdoch, speaking to shareholders in 2007, did admit that the road to success would be a long one. In many respects, CNBC is an even more established leader than CNN was at the time of the Fox News launch. "FBN faces many challenges, against an entrenched competitor with a seventeen-year head start. I view FBN's growth in terms of years, not months," Murdoch said.[35]

Plus, business news is a far more niche area of the news market than general news and politics. To be sure, Fox Business executives claimed that the new network would be more accessible to the average viewer than CNBC, and would be a place where corporate leaders could come on and share their stories and knowledge with the general public. But another channel dedicated to coverage of the economy and markets may now seem redundant. In fact, Wall Street became a big story at the time of Fox Business' launch. Because of the subprime mortgage crisis and slowing economy, financial stories were no longer an afterthought for CNN, Fox News and the major broadcast networks.

Federal Reserve Chairman Ben Bernanke used to be some-one that just day traders and hard-core Wall Street professionals cared about; but in the midst of the housing slump Bernanke often is a part of the lead story on CNN, Fox News and the network newscasts.

Even with Ailes, a CNBC veteran, on board to help build Fox Business, it may be difficult, if not impossible, for Fox Business to truly find a place for itself. After watching the network's first day of coverage, some Wall Street pros said they didn't see a need to keep watching, since it wasn't any different from CNBC. In fact, most who watched Fox Business on its first day were left wondering why there needed to be another business news network.

"It looks like the Saturday morning business shows on Fox News Channel. It's not that much different," said Barry Ritholtz, director of equity research for Fusion IQ, an asset management firm based in New York. "I was surprised when I heard that Fox wants to be more corporate friendly than CNBC. How much more corporate friendly can you get? I don't see where CNBC is bashing corporate executives. It is a pretty friendly environment for CEOs that want to come out and tell their story."[36]

To be fair, the network had both its low points and its high points in the first few days. The channel kicked off with coverage of industrial conglomerate Danaher's plans to buy testing and measuring equipment company Tektronix, an important story worth covering—but one that clearly meant more to investing professionals than to the Main Street viewer that Fox Business was claiming to target.

As the morning progressed, there was an interesting mix of features, ranging from an interview with skateboarder Tony

Hawk about his new video game to a service piece about how to take advantage of the weak dollar by investing in Asian currencies. But there was also a bizarre interview with the infamous self-proclaimed "Naked Cowboy" who strolls around New York's Times Square singing and playing his guitar in his underwear.

And, of course, Fox Business had the frenetic display of graphics that watchers of Fox News and just about all newscasts these days have grown accustomed to using. One investment professional said, however, that Fox Business risked going too far.

"The funny thing about Fox is their approach to news and sports to date has appeared to be more flash, graphics, sounds—a gluttony of sensory delight—and often I've worried it detracts from the content. That will be something they'll need to keep in mind as they look to target Wall Street professionals," said Todd Campbell, president of E. B. Capital Markets, an independent equity research firm serving professional investors based in Durham, New Hampshire.[37]

Still, Murdoch was not willing to throw in the towel on Fox Business despite some initial bad reviews. Speaking at a Bear Stearns media conference in March 2008, Murdoch reiterated that he was happy with the progress the network had made in its first few months and that as more cable systems picked up the channel, it would wind up eating into some of CNBC's audience. The key takeaway from his comments was that Murdoch still trusted Ailes completely and was not going to forget all the good that Ailes had done for News Corp.'s other cable networks. Bear Stearns has since been sold to JPMorgan Chase.

"I have total confidence in Roger Ailes. Fox Business is putting out a great-looking channel, especially in high-definition. What we have to do is get more distribution. But at the moment, we're happy with what we're doing," Murdoch said.[38]

He added that it will probably take two to three years for Fox Business to pay off. And in classic Murdoch style, he reminded the audience that Fox Business was not the first News Corp. venture to get off to a rough beginning before ultimately becoming a juggernaut. "People thought we were crazy with Fox News and Sky Italia," he said.[39]

Whether the idea was crazy or not, Fox Business is only one aspect of News Corp.'s broader cable plan, which is moving forward. Murdoch has set lofty targets for the company's international operations as well.

"The U.S. cable channels are just part of a web of successful channels we have around the world. The Fox International Channels -a business that didn't exist only a few years ago— grew its profits about 80 percent last year as it expanded to a larger global audience. Overall—including our operations at STAR and SKY Italia and elsewhere overseas, we now operate 270 channels, broadcasting in 31 languages, in more than 75 countries. And many of these channels are only beginning to show their potential. We have high hopes for all our channels in the coming years," Murdoch said.[40]

News Corp. is not ignoring the rest of the world. News Corp.

can trace its corporate roots to Australia and much of the success it has since enjoyed came through the healthy amounts of cash generated from Murdoch's Australian, and later British, publications. There would be no Fox broadcast channel, Fox News or Fox Business in the United States without Murdoch first altering the media landscape in Australia and Britain. And a closer look at how Murdoch came to dominate the satellite airwaves in the United Kingdom and Italy hint at what is yet to come from the company. Murdoch now has the rest of Europe and the even more lucrative markets in India, China and other parts of Asia in his crosshairs.

CHAPTER 4

The Sky's the Limit

News Corp. may be the only true global media company, perhaps because Murdoch's Australian roots and formative years in England have instilled in him a wider view of the world than that of many of his counterparts.

Large American media giants such as Walt Disney, CBS, Viacom, Time Warner and GE's NBC Universal certainly have a large presence worldwide, but they lack the scope of News Corp.'s global interests. Likewise, European and Asian media conglomerates such as Bertelsmann, Vivendi and Sony lack the presence in the United States that News Corp., which officially moved its headquarters from Australia to the United States in 2004, has.

In News Corp.'s fiscal year 2007, which ended in June of that year, the company generated nearly 32 percent of its total sales from Europe and 15 percent from Australia and Asia. Murdoch speaks proudly of his company's geographic diversification compared to that of his rivals. And as many media investors feared the possibility of a recession in the United States in early 2008, Murdoch sought to reassure Wall Street that his company could hold up much better in the event of a slowdown because it was not making bets solely on the United States.

"We are better positioned than other media companies to weather whatever comes. Our results are a powerful sign that our business is durable," Murdoch said during the company's fiscal second-quarter earnings conference call in February 2008. "We have a structurally more sound company with significantly lower exposure to the vagaries of the advertising market. Less than a quarter of our revenues are tied to the U.S. television advertising business."

Along those lines, operations outside of the United States have been booming for News Corp. in recent years. While total sales rose just 8.9 percent in the United States in fiscal 2007, revenues surged 17 percent in Australia and Asia and 20 percent throughout Europe.

David Bank, an analyst with RBC Capital Markets who covers media stocks, said News Corp.'s global exposure is one of the top reasons why the stock has, over time, outperformed most of its rivals'. He said Murdoch has a knack for finding the best opportunities in the right markets.

"They have strong international growth. News Corp. owns Sky Italia and they are just dominant. It is a massive growth engine for the company," Bank said.[1]

The expansion into satellite television was a crucial part of

Murdoch's strategy to diversify the company and make it less dependent on the vagaries of advertising. By the third quarter of fiscal 2008, Sky Italia accounted for 11 percent of News Corp.'s total sales and had finally begun to eke out an operating profit. What's more, revenues increased nearly 22 percent in the first nine months of the year, making the unit News Corp.'s second-fastest-growing operating division in terms of sales, trailing only the company's cable networks business. Meanwhile, at British Sky Broadcasting, which News Corp. owns a 39 percent stake in, revenues during the first nine months of fiscal 2008 rose 10 percent.

News Corp. is a minority investor in BSkyB, so its results are reported separately. News Corp. accounts for BSkyB's results as "equity affiliate investments."

But it was a long, painstaking process to build BSkyB and Sky Italia into the growth engines that they are today. And as will be discussed in more detail later, the decision to start BSkyB's predecessor, Sky Television, in 1988, combined with Murdoch's expensive shopping spree in the U.S. magazine business, almost killed the company. And along the way, Murdoch's satellite ambitions would make him an even more frequent target for those who felt that he was using News Corp.'s pervasive influence to unfairly garner preferential treatment from governments and regulators.

Murdoch first announced plans for Sky Broadcasting in 1988 and officially launched it in 1989. The network quickly reached 1 million viewers within a year, but the exorbitant amount of capital required to start and run a satellite television network nearly sent News Corp. into financial ruin. As a result, Murdoch was forced to abandon hopes of going it alone in the business and in 1990 Sky Television was merged with British Satellite Broadcasting to form British Sky Broadcasting, or BSkyB.

In 1994, News Corp. sold a stake in BSkyB to the public, reducing its ownership position in the company to about 40 percent and netting approximately $1.3 billion for News Corp. in the process. Once again, Murdoch was proving to investors that he had the Midas touch and that despite his company's near-bankruptcy a few years earlier, his penchant for taking big risks was paying off.

However, for the next few years, Murdoch would face some challenges in expanding his empire. What's more, his actions would provide even more fodder for those who felt he was using his role as one of the world's largest media giants unfairly to advance his interests.

In a precursor to News Corp.'s acquisition of Sky Italia, Murdoch first expressed interest in buying Italian television network Mediaset in 1998. In a move that would spark much controversy in Britain and throughout the European continent, Murdoch had British prime minister Tony Blair call Italian prime minister Romano Prodi to gauge Prodi's reaction to the possibility of a News Corp. takeover bid for Mediaset, which was controlled by Silvio Berlusconi, a former prime minister of Italy who would return to that position in 2001. (Ironically enough, Murdoch would later sell his yacht *Morning Glory* to Berlusconi.)

At first the British government denied that Blair had acted on Murdoch's behalf, but Murdoch eventually confessed that he did ask Blair to talk to Prodi. What's more, Murdoch showed no signs of guilt about doing so. "This was a perfectly innocent request for information which I would expect from any British business needing help from their government in European-wide investments," Murdoch said in a statement to the *Times*, which, lest we forget, is a News Corp.–owned paper.[2]

This embarrassed Blair and may have played a role in the British government's decision a year later to block Murdoch from realizing another one of his long-held dreams, taking control of the Manchester United soccer team.

In September 1998, BSkyB announced it was offering $1 billion to buy Manchester United, or ManU, as the team is known to its ardent supporters. The offer was the richest ever for a professional sports team and sent shock waves throughout both the media and sports worlds. Fans of the team were upset by the thought of Murdoch taking over. Many feared that he would look to move games from free television to pay television. This was most likely the main motivating factor behind the deal.

ManU is one of the world's most popular sports team franchises, topping even the storied New York Yankees in terms of recognition and reach among fans worldwide. But Murdoch wanted the team not necessarily for ego purposes, although that likely was part of it. Instead, ownership of ManU would have given BSkyB a leg up in renegotiating exclusive television broadcast rights with the Premier League, of which ManU was a member, when the current deal was set to expire in 2001.

Alas, the British government was not about to let Murdoch gain control of the nation's most well-known sports team. Blair and other leaders may have allowed Murdoch to whisper into their ears in the past, but they faced the risk of angering many potential voters if they approved the sale of the team to Murdoch. So the government could not afford to let the deal go through. In April 1999, Britain's secretary of state for the Department of Trade and Industry formally blocked the acquisition.

BSkyB expressed regrets about the decision but ultimately could do nothing more than accept defeat (not something Murdoch has ever gotten used to doing) and move on. "BSkyB is disappointed that the acquisition has been prevented from proceeding. BSkyB remains convinced it did not raise any competition or wider public interest concerns and that, had the acquisition proceeded, it would have been good for fans, good for football and good for Manchester United," the company said in a statement.[3]

At the same time that Murdoch was hitting some snags with BSkyB, News Corp. was also trying to become a leading satellite player in another soccer-mad nation: Italy. News Corp. had acquired a stake in a satellite television company there called Stream, which was launched in 1993 and co-owned by Telecom

Italia. But brutal competition in the Italian market from rival Telepiu, owned by Vivendi Universal and its Canal+ subsidiary, led to crippling losses for both satellite services.

With that in mind, News Corp. and Telecom Italia hammered out a deal to buy Telepiu from Vivendi. On October 1, 2002, the three companies announced that News Corp. and Telecom Italia would pay approximately $900 million for Telepiu and rename it Sky Italia. News Corp. would own 80.1 percent and Telecom Italia would own the remaining 19.9 percent.

Murdoch, speaking at his company's annual shareholder meeting in Adelaide, just eight days after sealing the deal to acquire Telepiu and form Sky Italia, described why he was so intent on becoming the leader in the Italian market. His remarks were yet another example of Murdoch's belief that acting in a bold, decisive way was the key to keeping the company's growth on track.

"This was a rare opportunity to form a single pay-TV platform in one of the world's wealthiest and most TV-passionate countries at an extremely attractive price," he said. "We see enormous growth potential for this platform. There is no cable in Italy, and free-to-air television is mediocre at best. By offering the richest collection of programming ever assembled on a single platform while eliminating the rampant piracy problem that has plagued operators in the past, we are confident of our ability to develop this service into another BSkyB, and to generate returns on our investment as early as the end of the next calendar year."[4]

The deal closed in April 2003. And during Murdoch's annual speech to shareholders at the company's investor meeting in October of that year, he boasted that Sky Italia would "one day be one of News Corp.'s shining jewels." He further predicted that Sky Italia would reach profitability within about a year and a half and that "it will have a very steep growth after that."[5]

"To say the least, we are all very excited about Sky Italia's prospects. I view Sky Italia's potential as being on a par with the world-class performance of our 35 percent-owned BSkyB," he concluded.[6]

In September 2004, News Corp. further cemented its grip on the market by agreeing to buy out the remaining 19.9 percent stake in Sky Italia from Telecom Italia. And the acquisition quickly paid off for Murdoch, just as he had expected. Sky Italia reported its first quarterly operating profit ever in the fourth quarter of fiscal 2005, which ended in June of that year. The unit posted a full-year operating profit of $39 million a year later.

With Murdoch building a leading presence in the United Kingdom and Italy, which accounted for 77 percent of News Corp.'s total sales throughout Europe in fiscal 2007, Murdoch then turned his sights on other parts of the continent. In January 2008, News Corp. once again embraced the German TV market, acquiring a 14.6 percent stake in Premiere AG, the largest cable TV operator in Germany and Austria, for about $423 million. In the next four months, News Corp. boosted its stake in Premiere three more times. It owned 25.1 percent as of May 2008.

"Pay TV is a core business for News Corporation and it's a category that's thriving across Europe with a multitude of new services and innovations. We see enormous potential for growth in Germany and believe the time is right to invest in its foremost pay-TV business, Premiere," said Murdoch in a statement.[7]

This was not the first time that Murdoch had invested in Premiere. News Corp. had done so in the late 1990s, buying a stake in Premiere's former parent KirchMedia in 1999, but was forced to take a nearly $1 billion loss on the investment in 2002, a loss that Murdoch dubbed a "black eye" at the time. The move to invest in Premiere again six years later was seen widely as a preemptive strike against Vivendi, which also was said to have taken an interest in acquiring part, or perhaps all, of Premiere.

Murdoch had also dabbled in Germany before through a joint venture with media giant and book publishing competitor Bertelsmann in 1994. News Corp. acquired a stake in German television station VOX that year from Bertelsmann but wound up selling it back in 1999 after enduring several years of losses.

But in financial circles, it is Murdoch's flirtations in Asia, particularly China, that have generated the most interest—and the most controversy.

In 1993, shortly after News Corp. announced that it was buying a controlling stake in the Asian television network STAR, Murdoch made a speech in London that angered the

Chinese government and set the stage for Murdoch's future tactics and strategies in dealing with China.

"Advances in the technology of communications have proved an unambiguous threat to totalitarian regimes. Fax machines enable dissidents to bypass state-controlled print media; direct-dial telephone makes it difficult for a state to control interpersonal voice communication; and satellite broadcasting makes it possible for information-hungry residents of many closed societies to bypass state-controlled television channels," Murdoch said in September 1993.[8]

The swift response from Beijing was to enact stricter regulations on satellite dishes in the country, a move that would obviously make it more difficult for STAR to do business.

Since then, Murdoch's actions toward the Chinese communist regime have raised eyebrows. Many who follow Murdoch believe that he has done everything possible to try to make amends with the government for his harsh remarks about "totalitarian regimes" in order to advance his business agenda in this potentially lucrative market.

The first such step to appease China was the removal of the British Broadcasting Corporation's international news channel from STAR's Chinese service because the Chinese government did not approve of a BBC program that was critical of former Chinese leader Mao Tse-Tung.

Soon after that, News Corp.'s HarperCollins book unit published *My Father Deng Xiaoping*, the English-language version of a biography of then Chinese leader Deng Xiaoping by his daughter Deng Rong, in 1995. This decision was proof to Murdoch's many critics that he would do whatever it took to get back in the good graces of the Chinese government.

"Murdoch handed over a million bucks to the daughter of Chinese Communist leader Deng Xiaoping for another Harper-Collins book for which commercial appeal barely extended beyond her immediate family. Of course the deal took place when Murdoch was hoping to receive official Chinese Communist approval to expand his satellite broadcasts into China. When he agreed to remove the BBC from Star TV's offering there, he explained, 'We're trying to get set up in China. Why should we upset them?' He later added, 'The truth is—and we Americans don't like to admit it—that authoritarian societies can work,' " wrote Eric Alterman, a senior fellow of the Center for American Progress, a self-described "progressive think-tank," on the organization's Web site in May 2007 after News Corp. announced its offer for Dow Jones.[9]

Two years after publishing the Deng Xiaoping biography, STAR agreed to air a twelve-hour documentary series on Deng Xiaoping that was produced by China Central Television (CCTV) and the Central Communist Party Document Research Department.

And finally, in 1998, HarperCollins pulled the plug on a widely hyped biography written by former Hong Kong governor Chris Patten, a critic of the communist government in China. That was viewed by many as perhaps the most egregious example of Murdoch using his authority to quash something that could have potentially alienated the Chinese government. The book, titled *East and West*, was eventually published later in 1998 by Macmillan in the United Kingdom and Crown, an imprint of Random House, in the United States.

Nine years after the flap over Patten's memoir, Murdoch admitted in an interview with *Time* magazine that he probably shouldn't have spiked the book. But in typical Murdoch fashion, he didn't express much remorse over the decision.

"I was probably in the wrong there too," Murdoch said in July 2007, during the height of the takeover battle for Dow Jones. "It's been a long career, and I've made some mistakes along the way. We're not all virgins."[10]

But the uproar over *East and West* would not be the last time Murdoch created controversy over what people perceived as kowtowing to China. In an article in *Vanity Fair* magazine in 1999, Murdoch spoke out against the Dalai Lama, the Buddhist spiritual leader who has received almost universal praise around the world but is the object of scorn to the Chinese communist regime because of his frequent criticism of China's continued occupation of Tibet.

"I have heard cynics who say he's a very political old monk shuffling around in Gucci shoes," Murdoch said about the Dalai Lama in the article. And later on in the story, he was quoted as suggesting that Tibet might be better off ruled by China. "It was a pretty terrible old autocratic society out of the Middle Ages," Murdoch said of Tibet.[11] "Maybe I'm falling for their propaganda," Murdoch added in the *Vanity Fair* piece, referring to the Chinese government, "but it was an authoritarian, medieval society without any basic services."[12]

For Murdoch, dealing with China has been a more complicated issue for personal reasons as well. Murdoch's third wife, Wendi Deng, was an executive for STAR in China who has since taken a more active role in working with MySpace in its efforts to expand into China. Murdoch married Deng, thirty-eight years his junior, in 1999, and she is the mother of Murdoch's two young daughters, Chloe and Grace. Murdoch even once joked in a speech in Tokyo that he is "an almost Asian with a Chinese wife."[13]

Another member of Murdoch's family has made his dealings in China even more complex. In 2001, Rupert's youngest son, James, who at the time was chairman and CEO of STAR, shocked people by declaring that many criticisms of the Chinese government were too harsh. James Murdoch went on to disparage Falun Gong, the Chinese spiritual movement that was treated by the government as a quasi-terrorist group and had been banned since the group held a protest in Tiananmen Square in 1999 to commemorate the ten-year anniversary of the prodemocracy rally in Tiananmen Square that ended with clashes between students and soldiers. James dubbed Falun Gong as "dangerous" and also called it an "apocalyptic cult" that "clearly does not have the success of China at heart."[14]

When James Murdoch stepped down as head of STAR in 2003 to take over as the chief executive officer of BSkyB, it appeared that critics would no longer have to worry about James having any influence in News Corp.'s Asian operations. They were wrong. In December 2007, James Murdoch was appointed News Corp.'s chairman and chief executive of Europe and Asia and was also renamed to News Corp.'s board. (James gave up his board seat in 2003 when he left News Corp. for BSkyB.) As part of James Murdoch's new role, he will oversee, according to a statement from News Corp., "the strategic and operational development of News Corporation's television, newspaper and related digital assets in Europe, Asia and the Middle East."[15] That obviously includes STAR as well as News Corp.'s growing Internet presence, particularly with MySpace, in China. What's more, the decision to name James Murdoch the head of all of News Corp.'s European and Asian businesses was widely interpreted by analysts and media observers that Rupert Murdoch wants James eventually to succeed him as News Corp.'s chairman and CEO.

This development, along with News Corp.'s purchase of Dow Jones in 2007, reignited fears about Murdoch and his business affairs in China. One of the critic's biggest concerns was how Murdoch might attempt to influence coverage of China in Dow Jones' publications, most notably the prestigious *Wall Street Journal.*

However, the first big test of how the new Dow Jones might report on China, ironically enough, didn't involve the *Journal*, but a far smaller publication. And the source of the controversy wasn't necessarily the Chinese government but Murdoch himself.

In early 2008, the book *Rupert's Adventures in China: How Murdoch Lost a Fortune and Found a Wife* was published. The book was written by Bruce Dover, a former Murdoch associate who during the 1990s was a News Corp. vice president based in Beijing.

The book, which had already been reviewed in many business publications in Asia and Europe, was set to be reviewed in a small monthly out of Hong Kong called the *Far Eastern Economic Review*. But that publication was owned by Dow Jones, and hence Murdoch.

According to an account in the *International Herald Tribune* from February 2008, Hugo Restall, the editor of the *Far Eastern Economic Review*, originally assigned a review of the book to a freelancer but changed his mind about publishing the review after it was filed when he realized that the book was casting his new boss in an unfavorable light and also devoted a lot of time to Murdoch's wooing of and subsequent marriage to Wendi Deng.[16]

Restall, in e-mails to Eric Ellis, the Australian freelance journalist based in Jakarta who was set to write the review, wrote that "I'm afraid I am getting cold feet on this one—I've just gotten a copy of the book, and it looks more like the work of a disgruntled ex-employee, rather than an analysis of the business." He apologized to Ellis for deciding not to publish the review and added that he "should have looked at the book first."[17]

It was not made clear if Murdoch actually had a hand in

killing the review. But it's doubtful the publication even registered a blip on Murdoch's radar, given that the *Far Eastern Economic Review*, which claims on its Web site that it has a circulation of just over 12,500 subscribers, isn't exactly a well-known or well-read magazine.

Nonetheless, Restall's admission of "cold feet" and his decision not to publish the review out of fear of how Murdoch might view it is a stark reminder that even if Murdoch does not officially meddle in the editorial affairs of his publications, the fact that he has a reputation as someone who would look to do so has an effect on his employees and how they run their businesses.

Readers of his publications, including his newly acquired Dow Jones newspapers, probably have legitimate reason to be concerned that coverage of China could be affected. But Richard Dorfman of the media investment firm Richard Alan believes some of the talk about Murdoch having a possibly deleterious effect on the paper is overblown.

"The average reader is not going to stop reading the *Wall Street Journal* or read it with a different vantage point because they think Murdoch is polluting it. I don't think the fact that he owns the paper will affect the potential number of visitors to the WSJ.com Web site. The publication will continue to get readers from around the world interested in investing opportunities and making money," Dorfman said. "Murdoch views the *Wall Street Journal* as having tremendous opportunities overseas.

People in Eastern Europe or other growth areas are not going to stop going to the site on principle. His history, his background, his politics and his ideology will not affect in any monetary way his businesses. They will live or die and suffer or prosper on their own merits."[18]

Still, it will be up to Murdoch to prove the naysayers wrong by allowing the *Wall Street Journal* and other Dow Jones publications the freedom to publish stories and opinion pieces that are both critical of him and the Chinese government.

As China's market continues to open up and Murdoch looks to do more business there—not just with STAR but through his expanding portfolio of Internet assets such as MySpace—it will be crucial for Murdoch to live up to the promise of editorial independence that he made when acquiring Dow Jones.

The tenor of Murdoch's comments in a speech made in Tokyo in November 2006 sounded more like those made in 1993 that originally got him in hot water with the Chinese government than the often mollifying remarks he had made in the years immediately following his "totalitarian regimes" speech.

He urged the Chinese government to open up even more to the West. "We all know that the rise of Asia has only been made possible by this region engaging with the world. Without the 'open door' policy, China would still be an inward-looking, underdeveloped country whose talented people were far from fulfilling their potential. In the past three decades China has reclaimed its greatness by reopening itself to the world. It is a vivid example of why we must ensure that the nations of the world are open to business and open to each other," he said.[19]

Later on in his speech, Murdoch tackled the issue of a free press in Asia and suggested that the region's governments needed to be as accommodating to the media as the governments of Western nations are. "Is freedom of the press the privilege of a few countries or the right of all? Should the flow of information on the Internet be blocked? And who should do the blocking? Can a barricade be built against the world outside? As Asia has developed, there has been a vigorous debate about values. Some have argued that the West has tried to impose its values on this region," he said, before concluding that "a free press also holds companies, governments and individuals to account. Accountability is not a Western value. It is a necessary condition for success."[20]

Murdoch added that "globalization is real and it has been overwhelmingly beneficial. 'Globalization' is not a word we should be ashamed of," and concluded by urging China to be as flexible as India in order to ensure that China could wind up enjoying the same type of long-term economic prosperity as India.[21]

"There is a vigorous debate about the relative strengths and weaknesses of China and India. But one fact is beyond debate. The free flow of information is a crucial advantage in an ultra-competitive world. There is no doubt that India is producing thousands of managers who are capable of running any company anywhere in the world. There is also no doubt that these impressive managers would not be developed in such impressive numbers if India attempted to dam the flow of facts or of opinion," he said.[22]

"These are sophisticated individuals who will be role models for coming generations. Change moves swiftly in our digitally compressed age. The speed of information magnifies differences and highlights conflict. Yet I believe that the more we know about each other, the more we understand how much we have in common. And a free press is crucial to that process," Murdoch added.[23]

So is this merely a case of Murdoch trying to show his detractors that he's mellowed as he's aged? Probably not. These more liberal (at least for Murdoch) remarks are not likely to stop Murdoch's legion of critics from questioning how he will use his various media properties to promote his interests in China and elsewhere around the globe. They will continue to look for signs of Murdoch using his influence in an unfair manner. And given how prone to controversy the outspoken Murdoch is, the skeptics probably will be able to find evidence of something they don't approve of more often than not.

CHAPTER 5

Wheeling and Dealing

Part of what makes Murdoch so fascinating—besides his willingness to speak bluntly while so many other media executives shun controversy—is his constant need to be involved in a deal.

It is a rare time when News Corp. isn't actively buying or selling something. And while this strategy has obviously helped transform News Corp. from a simple Australian newspaper publisher to a global media titan, the ceaseless deal activity has occasionally gotten Murdoch into trouble with investors, especially those who prefer he slow down and stop burning through so much cash.

Murdoch conceded as much during remarks at a Goldman Sachs media conference in September 2007, joking that his stock occasionally underperforms that of other media rivals such as Walt Disney, Time Warner and Viacom because investors worry about what deal he is going to make next. "There's a

Murdoch discount because everyone thinks I'll go buy something," he quipped.[1]

More often than not, Murdoch's impulsiveness has served him well. One can argue that if he spent more time analyzing whether his company needed to expand, he would have missed out on buying MySpace. If he had been more afraid of failure, he may have never decided to start Fox or Fox News. Those who follow Murdoch closely say that even though he has a reputation for moving quickly, and perhaps too quickly at times, his flexibility to make snap decisions has helped make News Corp. the juggernaut it is today.

"Strategically, Murdoch has been ahead of everybody. He's been looking at everything from a more global perspective than anyone else in the media business," said Alan Gould, an analyst who follows News Corp. for Wall Street investment bank Natixis Bleichroeder.[2]

Along those lines, Murdoch is one of the few remaining media moguls who has an active say, if not the only say, in how his company is run. That is not the case at most other media giants, probably because, unlike News Corp., they are not controlled predominantly by one family or large group of allied shareholders.

Even the two that are, Sumner Redstone–controlled CBS and Viacom, are run in a far different fashion. Redstone split Viacom into two separately traded public companies in 2006. CBS, in addition to the flagship television network, owns a giant radio and outdoor advertising business, the cable network

Showtime and book publisher Simon & Schuster. Viacom owns the Paramount movie studio and youth-oriented cable networks such as MTV, Nickelodeon and Comedy Central.

While Redstone is still the chairman of both CBS and Viacom and is the companies' controlling shareholder, he is far less active in the day-to-day management and decision making at both companies than Murdoch is at News Corp. Longtime CBS television chief Leslie Moonves is the CEO of CBS and, in the eyes of Wall Street analysts and institutional investors, is the most prominent executive at the firm. Meanwhile, at Viacom, Redstone entrusted Philippe Dauman, who had been a Viacom executive from 1993 to 2000, to call the shots. Dauman, who had left to form his own private equity firm, was brought back by Redstone in September 2006 to replace then-CEO Tom Freston.

There has also been a high degree of turmoil in the executive suites at News Corp.'s other major media competitors. Walt Disney's longtime CEO Michael Eisner faced callings for his ouster in the earlier part of this decade after ratings at ABC slumped and Disney's stock began to underperform compared to other media companies. Eisner ultimately was forced to step down as CEO and chairman before his contract expired, following a massive vote of no confidence at the company's annual shareholder meeting in 2004.

Eisner was succeeded by Disney veteran Robert Iger, who has been the polar opposite of Eisner and, in many respects, Murdoch. Iger has been more of a peacemaker than an antagonist, repairing Disney's tattered relationship with longtime partner Pixar, the computer animation studio founded by Apple's Steve Jobs.

Disney eventually acquired Pixar, and as a result of that deal Jobs became a Disney board member and the company's largest shareholder. The newfound spirit of cooperation between Disney and Jobs helped Disney gain a genuine edge over other media companies in the digital media market, as Disney was the first major studio to allow its television shows, and later movies, to be sold on Apple's popular iTunes site. News Corp. eventually followed suit, inking deals with Apple for TV show sales in May 2006 and movie sales and rentals in January 2008.

Another of News Corp.'s top media rivals, Time Warner, also had a drastically different corporate culture and management style. Time Warner, which was built through a series of mergers that created a complicated and top-heavy management system, was an organization that many media analysts and investors ridiculed as being too sluggish to act.

Activist investor and Time Warner shareholder Carl Icahn called for Time Warner to be broken up into four companies in 2006, citing frustration with the company's poor stock performance when compared to rivals like News Corp. and Disney. "A great company in the media business needs visionary leaders, not a conglomerate structure headquartered in Columbus Circle that second-guesses," Icahn said at the time he proposed his overhaul of Time Warner.[3]

Icahn eventually called off plans to elect his own slate of

directors to carry out his breakup plan. And ironically enough, Time Warner's new chief executive officer Jeffrey Bewkes, who took over for Richard Parsons in January 2008, may wind up following Icahn's advice. Time Warner has agreed to spin off its Time Warner Cable division and Bewkes suggested Time Warner will split its struggling AOL business into two units, which may make it easier for AOL to be sold.

Murdoch, however, has rarely faced opposition or challenges to his leadership. This combined with the advice of his trusted lieutenant Peter Chernin, gives News Corp. an advantage over competitors, according to investors.

"News Corp. is run by two strong executives. They make it work," said Morris Mark, president of Mark Asset Management, a New York–based hedge fund. Mark said that when News Corp. wants to make a bold move, Murdoch just goes ahead and throws caution to the wind.[4]

To that end, Murdoch acts quickly when he is faced with mounting criticism from shareholders and analysts. For example, Mark said that when Time Warner finally decided in 2005 to stop charging AOL's broadband subscribers a monthly fee, that was a move that most media observers said was months, if not years, overdue. But if Murdoch owned AOL, Mark said it wouldn't have taken nearly as long to come to that decision. "I don't think Murdoch would have had a committee meeting. He would have just done it."[5]

And to Murdoch's credit, even when he was busy buying properties only to sell them later on, he often did so at great benefit to the company's shareholders. Murdoch sold the alternative New York weekly magazine the *Village Voice* in 1985 for $55 million after buying it in 1977 for only $7.6 million. Murdoch was able to use some of the proceeds from the *Village Voice* sale to help finance the launch of the Fox broadcast network a year later. News Corp. bought the *Chicago Sun-Times* in 1983 for $90 million and sold the tabloid three years later for $145 million.

Most recently, in 1997, News Corp.'s Fox Kids Worldwide, a joint venture between News Corp. and children's programming syndicator Saban Corp., acquired International Family Entertainment Inc., a cable channel owned by televangelist Pat Robertson, for $1.9 billion. News Corp. and Saban then turned around in 2001 and sold the company, by that time known as Fox Family Worldwide, to Walt Disney for $5.2 billion in cash and assumed debt.

He's also made savvy investments that have complemented other News Corp. businesses. Shares of NDS, a technology company founded in Israel that News Corp. owned about 72 percent of until the company was taken private in 2008, nearly doubled since NDS went public in 1999. News Corp. and private equity firm Permira agreed to take NDS private in June. News Corp. reduced its stake in NDS to 49 percent as part of the transaction, selling a portion of NDS to Permira for about $1.7 billion.

"This is an undiscovered gem," said Daniel Meron, an analyst with RBC Capital Markets in March 2007. "It's extremely well positioned in a growth market and has an excellent management team. But few people know of it."[6]

NDS, which has headquarters in the United Kingdom and New York, develops technology such as digital TV smart cards that store consumer-viewing information, software for cable set-top boxes and digital video recorders for cable, satellite and phone companies across the globe. In that regard, NDS competes with the likes of TiVo as well as subsidiaries of technology giants Motorola and Cisco Systems.

The company's biggest customer is DirecTV, which had, up until 2008, been a sizable News Corp. investment. NDS replaced TiVo as the exclusive supplier of digital video recorders for new DirecTV subscribers in 2005. After DirecTV, NDS's next biggest customers are BSkyB and Sky Italia. In other words, Murdoch essentially has an in-house supplier of cutting-edge technology, which means he doesn't have to go out and negotiate with the likes of TiVo, Motorola and Cisco.

Nonetheless, Murdoch's freewheeling ways and bold acquisitions haven't always helped the company. He has often made purchases that he's had to backtrack on after only a few years.

Most notably, Murdoch's aggressive acquisition spree in the late 1980s almost led News Corp. to financial ruin. In 1988, the company acquired Triangle Publications, the media firm owned by philanthropist Walter Annenberg, for nearly $3 billion. At the time, this was News Corp.'s biggest acquisition to date and several analysts, not surprisingly, felt Murdoch was overpaying for the company.

But Murdoch saw value in Triangle's stable of magazines, particularly *TV Guide*, which many critics worried Murdoch would use to unfairly promote Fox programming over that of other networks. Triangle also owned the *Daily Racing Form* and *Seventeen* magazines.

However, the Triangle acquisition came only one year after Murdoch made several other large deals, including the purchase of book publisher Harper & Row for $300 million, the *South China Morning Post* newspaper for about $230 million as well as a minority stake in Pearson, the publisher of the *Financial Times* (and the owner of the publisher of this book, the Penguin Group).

Spending a lot of money on acquisitions wasn't Murdoch's only cross to bear. Murdoch was aggressively acquiring at a time when he was also investing heavily in his start-up satellite television businesses around the world, investments that required a lot of up-front capital.

In 1989, News Corp. launched Sky Television in the United Kingdom. In order to fund this expansion as well as the Triangle acquisition, Murdoch was forced to go heavily into debt, precisely at the wrong time. That's because global credit markets were in turmoil due to banks' exposure to bad real estate loans.

By 1990, News Corp. had more than $7 billion in debt and more than a third of that was short-term debt due within a year. There was wild speculation that Murdoch might have to conduct a fire sale to meet his debt obligations and that even assets such as the Fox network and movie studio or HarperCollins could ultimately be dumped. Shares of News Corp.'s publicly traded shares on the New York Stock Exchange (which were first listed in 1987) plunged nearly 75 percent between mid-July 1990 and January 2001.

Ultimately, because creditors renegotiated a large part of the debt, Murdoch was saved from needing to do a massive purge of his most attractive assets or, worse, having to declare bankruptcy. Murdoch was also able to ease the competitive strains facing Sky Television by merging it with rival British Satellite Broadcasting to create British Sky Broadcasting, or BSkyB, with News Corp. controlling half of the new entity.

But Murdoch did have to give up much of what he bought from Triangle only a few years earlier. In 1991, News Corp. sold *Seventeen* and the *Daily Racing Form* as well as several other magazines it had acquired in the past few years, including *New York, Soap Opera Digest, Soap Opera Weekly* and *Premiere* to Primedia for about $650 million. He also sold off most of the trade publications he had acquired in the 1980s, as well as most of his U.S. newspapers.

Murdoch had avoided a complete catastrophe and he would be wary of adding too much debt to fund his empire-building ambitions in the future. But not even near-bankruptcy could get Murdoch to completely change his acquisitive ways.

"Do I think he's learned from his mistakes? I don't know if he has. A leopard really can't change his spots," says Dorfman. "He's an amazing visionary, even at this stage of his career. He has his pulse on the industry and can see things down the road that most of us can't. But that can be a double-edged sword. He is bit of a gambler. He has no hesitation to load up on debt and never has. And it's bitten him a few times."[7]

Still, it would be several years after selling much of the publishing business before News Corp.'s balance sheet and stock price completely recovered. But by the mid-1990s, Murdoch was once again ready to resume his deal making and heavy investments. And once again, some of those purchases and deals worked out better than others.

In 1993, the company paid approximately $525 million for a controlling stake in Hong Kong–based STAR, a leading broad cast television provider in Asia. The unit, along with Murdoch's large satellite divisions Sky Italia and BSkyB, grew dramatically under News Corp.'s ownership and was a significant part of News Corp.'s success internationally.

But by 2007, STAR's growth, particularly in India, had slowed down somewhat, prompting Murdoch to clean house. In January 2007, News Corp. announced that STAR CEO Michelle Guthrie, who had led the network for more than six years, was stepping down and would be replaced by Paul Aiello, a former Morgan Stanley investment banker who had joined STAR in 2006.

Shortly after Guthrie's departure, News Corp. announced that the two top executives of STAR India, Peter Mukerjea and Sameer Nair, were also leaving the company.

The shake-up would be completed later in 2007 when News Corp. announced that Murdoch's youngest son James, who had been CEO of BSkyB since 2003, would become the new chairman and CEO of News Corp.'s Europe and Asia operations, giving him the responsibility to oversee STAR, News International UK, Sky Italia and News Corporation Europe. James Murdoch had previously been the chairman and CEO of STAR from 2000 to 2003.

Speaking at a Citigroup investment conference in January 2008, Peter Chernin candidly described the changes at STAR as necessary to get the unit's growth back on track. He talked about how the company became complacent, particularly in India, because of its leadership position. That led to STAR losing market share to top rival ZEE Television.

"We made some mistakes and did some stupid things and acknowledged them. We had been underinvesting in new channels. When you are a dominant player in an emerging landscape, this is not the time to milk your success. This is one of the great growth areas in the world and it is a land grab right now. There are plenty of opportunities in India and we want to be the number one media company there within the next few years," Chernin said.[8]

The problems at STAR were a rare example of Murdoch losing focus on an emerging market. But he did move swiftly to address slowing growth before conditions got to a point where it was no longer economically viable for him to remain a big player in India.

But Murdoch was not so lucky with forays into other businesses during the late 1990s and the early part of the 2000s, leading some media observers to once again wonder if Murdoch hadn't overextended News Corp.

In 1998, the company's Fox group subsidiary bought the Los Angeles Dodgers baseball team from the O'Malley family, who originally earned lifetime scorn from the residents of Brooklyn for moving the team out of that New York City borough to California in 1957, for $311 million.

But News Corp. struggled to make money from the Dodgers and, compounding matters, the team made some curious personnel moves that angered many of its loyal fans.

Under Murdoch's ownership, the Dodgers traded star catcher Mike Piazza to the Florida Marlins in May 1998. The team also fired manager Bill Russell, who had spent his entire eighteen-year career as a player for the team, in June 1998. In December of that year, the team signed pitcher Kevin Brown to a seven-year, $105 million contract, making him, at the time, the first major league player with a long-term deal in excess of $100 million.

Many sportswriters, probably taking their cues from the financial press, immediately branded the signing as exorbitant for a player who many believed was past his prime. Brown pitched well in his first year with the Dodgers, but injuries took their toll on him after that, limiting his effectiveness. He was subsequently traded to the New York Yankees in 2003 and several baseball writers have since dubbed the Brown deal as one of the worst free-agent signings in the sport's history.

After six seasons of mediocrity—the Dodgers had a record

of 509–463 from 1998 through 2003 and never made it to the playoffs in any of those seasons—News Corp. wound up agreeing to sell the team in October 2003 to Boston real estate developer Frank McCourt.

Although News Corp. was able to sell the team for far more than what it had paid for it—$430 million—it's not as if Murdoch could crow to shareholders that he had generated a nice return to them. After all, News Corp. spent about $50 million on renovating Dodger Stadium while the company owned it. In addition, News Corp. claimed that it lost more than $60 million a year on the team during its five years of ownership. Dodger Blue bled red ink for Murdoch.

What's more, one of the major points behind owning the Dodgers was to give News Corp. control of more programming that could help News Corp. turn its regional group of cable sports networks into a legitimate national contender against Walt Disney's national sports juggernaut ESPN. While the regional sports networks have continued to post strong results for News Corp., Fox Sports still cannot match the power and profitability of ESPN. So it's hard to consider News Corp.'s five-year foray into professional sports ownership as a success.

The Dodgers experiment is in many ways a perfect example of how Murdoch sometimes buys businesses that he does not understand, companies that do not deliver the type of financial results his stockholders have come to expect from Murdoch's core businesses. And it is also a testament to Murdoch's willingness to take huge risks. But with huge risks often come huge failures. Nowhere was that more evident than with News Corp.'s money-losing investment in *TV Guide*.

TV Guide was the one magazine that Murdoch acquired from Triangle Publications in 1988 that he wound up holding on to following his need-for-cash-induced mass exodus from the magazine publishing business in 1991.

But in 1998, Murdoch finally gave up some control of the publication, agreeing to sell it to United Video Satellite Group, a leading provider of interactive on-screen television listing guides, for $2 billion. As part of that deal, News Corp. received a 40 percent equity stake, representing a 48 percent voting interest in the new company, which was later renamed TV Guide Inc.

The other major shareholder in the new entity was Tele-Communications Inc.'s Liberty Media unit, a media company controlled by onetime ally and soon-to-be rival John Malone, the chairman of Liberty Media. Just a few months later, TV Guide Inc. was acquired by United Video Satellite's top rival Gemstar, in a deal worth a staggering $9.2 billion. This gave News Corp. a 20 percent stake in the combined company, which was later renamed Gemstar–TV Guide.

At the time, Murdoch looked like a genius. On paper, he was able to finally prove that his gut instinct to buy *TV Guide* from Annenberg in 1988 was a good one. And in September 2000, News Corp. and Malone's Liberty Media agreed to a complex stock swap that gave News Corp. ownership of Liberty's stake in Gemstar–TV Guide. That deal boosted News Corp.'s interest in Gemstar–TV Guide to a little more than 40 percent, a stake valued at the time at around $12 billion.

Murdoch viewed the investment in Gemstar as a way to dominate the "new media" equivalent of *TV Guide* as more television watchers relied on electronic guides to find programming than on magazines like *TV Guide* or television listings in local newspapers.

"The world is just now beginning to appreciate the power and capability of Gemstar's patented electronic programming guide," Murdoch said in a conference call with reporters and analysts. "Our increased ownership in Gemstar–TV Guide gives us the opportunity to gain a controlling stake over the management of that company in the future, as well as a greater stake in what we believe will be a great growth industry."[9]

But Murdoch didn't have long to celebrate. Gemstar–TV Guide's stock, along with many other technology and media stocks, plunged in the wake of the tech, telecom and dot-com bust in late 2000. Gemstar's shares went from trading around $90 in October 2000 to a low of $2.55 a share in September 2002. As a result of the stock's stunning plunge, News Corp. took about a $6 billion write-down on its investment in Gemstar–TV Guide in 2002.

Making matters worse, allegations of accounting shenanigans started to dog Gemstar's CEO Henry Yuen in 2002. Yuen was fired in 2003 and he and other Gemstar officers were formally accused by the Securities and Exchange Commission in 2003 of inflating the company's revenues between March 2000 and September 2002. Yuen was found liable for securities fraud in 2006.

This was an embarrassing blow for Murdoch, who described Yuen in a March 2001 issue of *BusinessWeek* as "a brilliant strategist" who "has shown to have a novel way for thinking out of the box."[10] Gemstar's stock never recovered from the accounting scandal and Murdoch finally extricated himself from the Gemstar–TV Guide debacle in 2007. In July of that year, the company put itself up for sale and in December of that year, copyright protection software maker Macrovision agreed to buy the company for $2.8 billion, meaning that News Corp.'s stake was worth only about $1.1 billion.

One analyst suggested Murdoch's willingness to finally throw in the towel on Gemstar was a signal to investors that he was man enough to admit his mistakes. After all, investors were growing increasingly skeptical of his $5 billion bid for Dow Jones. So the decision to dump an investment—even at a loss—was welcome news. It demonstrated that Murdoch realized scaling back in some noncore areas was the right thing to do at a time when he was expanding elsewhere.

"It's hard to separate Gemstar's decision to sell from what's going on at News Corp. While I don't think the Dow Jones bid is a major driving force behind this, Murdoch may be looking to offset the view on Wall Street about him being acquisition crazy," said Alan Gould, an analyst with investment bank Natixis Bleichroeder.[11]

But strangely enough, the massive loss associated with *TV*

Guide probably wasn't the worst part of Murdoch's ill-fated investment in Gemstar. Rather, the Gemstar deal opened the door for John Malone to gain a greater stake in News Corp., an investment that he possibly could have used to wrest control of the company away from Murdoch and his family. Murdoch wasn't about to let that happen. But the ultimate sacrifice for keeping Malone at bay was that News Corp. would have to abandon its efforts to gain a foothold in the lucrative U.S. satellite television market only a few years after entering it.

For Murdoch, there would be no repeat of the success of BSkyB and Sky Italia in America.

Here is how, thanks to his willingness to give too much of a stake to Malone, Murdoch assembled and then quickly was forced to sell News Corp.'s controlling stake in DirecTV, an asset that Murdoch had craved for years.

In April 1999, Murdoch agreed to swap a stake in News Corp. to Malone's Liberty Media in exchange for Malone's 50 percent interest in the Fox/Liberty group of regional sports networks. In a separate transaction, Malone agreed to buy the 5 percent stake in News Corp. owned by telecommunications firm MCI. All told, the two deals gave Malone an 8 percent stake in News Corp. At the time, Murdoch did not seem concerned about having Malone as such a significant investor.

"We're particularly pleased to have the confidence of John Malone. For a long time, Dr. Malone has been the most successful strategist in our industry. His decision to accept News

[Corp.] stock in consideration for their ownership position is the strongest possible endorsement of our current strategic direction as well as our future prospects," Murdoch said in a statement in April 1999.[12]

In fact, Murdoch was even willing to give Malone more control of the company so News Corp. could gain a greater stake in Gemstar–TV Guide. As part of the September 2000 deal that involved News Corp. acquiring Liberty's stake in Gemstar–TV Guide, News Corp. exchanged approximately 121.5 million nonvoting shares of News Corp. to Malone, thereby boosting his ownership in News Corp. to 20 percent and making Malone the company's second-largest shareholder behind the Murdoch family.

Malone and Murdoch would continue to coexist peacefully for the next year or so, which allowed Murdoch to begin his quest to acquire a controlling stake in U.S. satellite television broadcaster DirecTV from General Motors' Hughes Corporation.

Given the success of BSkyB and Sky Italia, it was a no-brainer for Murdoch to try and replicate that success in the country he now officially called home.

In 1997, News Corp. proposed to buy a 40 percent stake in EchoStar Communications, the operator of the DISH Network. EchoStar founder Charlie Ergen agreed to the deal but News Corp. backed out after it appeared that U.S. regulators would not approve it. EchoStar subsequently sued News Corp.

for $5 billion and News Corp. countersued. The two companies settled in 1998, with News Corp. receiving 24 million new shares of EchoStar stock in exchange for two satellites.

The two companies were at it again in 2001. Each bid for Hughes, but Hughes spurned News Corp. Hughes decided in favor of Ergen's bid. However, the Federal Communications Commission and Department of Justice both refused to approve the deal due to antitrust concerns. Many religious broadcasters voiced heavy opposition to the deal. They argued that a merger between Hughes and EchoStar would create a monopoly that would limit the amount of religious programming available on satellite television. Critics of Murdoch have alleged that he was one of the main mobilizing forces behind the intense lobbying against the deal.

But in April 2003, Murdoch finally succeeded in winning a coveted piece of the U.S. satellite market. He announced that News Corp. was buying a 19.9 percent stake in Hughes Electronics, a separately traded General Motors subsidiary, from GM. He was also buying another 14.1 percent from other public shareholders and GM pension plans, for $6.6 billion in cash and stock. The combined 34 percent stake in Hughes would effectively give News Corp. and its Fox subsidiary control of Hughes' DirecTV unit, the nation's largest satellite television provider. Upon closing the deal, News Corp. planned to transfer the Hughes stake to Fox Entertainment Group, a separately traded stock that News Corp. spun off in 1998 and owned more than 80 percent of.

Murdoch glowed about the deal and immediately predicted that News Corp.'s success in the satellite television business abroad would translate to similar success in the United States. "The benefits will be felt almost immediately—in the competition it will offer cable, the richer services it will provide to American viewers, and the value it will create for the shareholders of Fox, News Corp. and Hughes," he said in a press release.[13]

Murdoch continued to wax rhapsodic about the deal and it appeared that he was viewing this as his most significant acquisition to date.

"With Fox taking a significant interest in Hughes, we are forging what we believe will be the premier diversified entertainment company in America today, with leading assets in film, television broadcasting and production, cable programming, and now pay-TV distribution," he concluded.[14]

But Murdoch also knew that he would face an uphill battle getting the deal approved by U.S. regulators. There had already been opposition to his plans to buy a stake in EchoStar. What's more, Murdoch's role in helping to get the EchoStar-Hughes deal killed clearly made Ergen even more of a foe and it was highly likely that Ergen would argue vociferously against Murdoch and News Corp. being allowed to gain a controlling stake in his top rival.

Realizing this, Murdoch quickly went on the offensive to tout the potential benefits of the Hughes deal to U.S. consumers in an attempt to mitigate any concerns that News Corp.'s rapidly growing media empire would be harmful to competition.

"The alignment of Fox's valuable content assets and Direc-TV's distribution platform will provide significant benefits to consumers and greatly enhance the future businesses of both companies. With almost fifteen years of expertise gained at our worldwide pay-TV platforms, including the industry-leading BSkyB, we are confident in our ability to grow this asset quickly, rewardingly and in a manner consistent with the competitive spirit that has guided News Corp. for half a century. From day one, we have pledged to make our programming available to all multichannel distributors on nondiscriminatory prices, terms and conditions, and at the same time to open the DirecTV platform to all competing programmers," Murdoch said the day of the Hughes deal announcement.[15]

Ultimately, Murdoch did not have a difficult time convincing regulators that the deal should be approved. And on December 19, 2003, the Department of Justice and Federal Communications Commission both gave their blessing to the transaction. The purchase closed three days later. Murdoch finally had what he'd desired for the last several years: access to the U.S. satellite-TV distribution market. This was a lucrative business in and of itself but also a means for giving Murdoch and News Corp.'s cable programming assets, such as Fox News, FX and its regional sports channels, an important ally in negotiating favorable carriage deals.

Murdoch was giddy about finally gaining control of a U.S. satellite business. In his remarks to shareholders at the company's annual shareholder meeting two months before receiving approval for the deal, he said that "the anticipated completion of the DirecTV transaction will mark the culmination of a long-time pursuit by our company of providing the missing link in a global satellite television platform that will span four continents and encompass 23 million subscribers at its beginning, all of which will give us, I believe, the perfect balance of assets for a media company, the right mix of subscription and advertising revenues, the right mix of content and distribution businesses, and a geographic breadth that is unmatched by any media company in the world today."[16]

But a couple of strange things happened shortly after News Corp.'s purchase of the controlling stake in DirecTV closed. Competition in the cable and satellite television market became much more intense than Murdoch had ever imagined and Murdoch's old friend John Malone started acting like a shareholder who had more than just a passive interest in the running of the company.

When News Corp. acquired its stake in Hughes Electronics, which was subsequently renamed the DirecTV Group, Murdoch envisioned that DirecTV would be able to effectively compete against cable in the broadband Internet access market.

In testimony to the U.S. House Committee on the Judiciary during a hearing about competition in the satellite television industry in May 2003, Murdoch spoke about how News Corp. planned to be a leader in making high-speed Internet services available to subscribers.

"News Corp. will work aggressively to build on the services

already provided by Hughes to make broadband available throughout the United States, particularly in rural areas. Broadband solutions for all Americans could come from partnering with other satellite broadband providers, DSL providers, or new potential broadband providers using broadband over power line systems, or from other emerging technologies. News Corp. believes it is critical that consumers have vibrant broadband choices that compete with cable's video and broadband services on capability, quality and price," Murdoch said.[17]

Along those lines, DirecTV and telecom giant Verizon Communications announced a partnership in January 2004 in which Verizon would offer phone and Internet packages that also included satellite television service from DirecTV. EchoStar had a similar arrangement in place with SBC Communications, the Baby Bell phone company that would later acquire AT&T as well as BellSouth and rename itself AT&T.

The problem for Murdoch, though, was that the phone companies were not content with merely packaging satellite television service alongside their phone and high-speed digital subscriber line (DSL) Internet access services. Leading cable companies such as Comcast, Time Warner Cable, Cox, Charter Communications and Cablevision were busy launching an assault on Verizon and AT&T's customers by offering their own digital phone services in addition to their standard video service and broadband high-speed Internet access.

This so-called triple play of telephone, video and Internet

access was a compelling offer for many consumers and the phone companies decided to strike back, not only in order to stem losses they were facing in their bread-and-butter phone business but also to try and steal away cable's video and broadband customers.

In 2005, Verizon launched its own television service known as FiOS TV, which ran over a fiber-optic network that Verizon spent billions of dollars to build out. Likewise, AT&T (still known as SBC at the time) was busy preparing its own fiberoptic television offering known as U-verse. Suddenly the need for phone companies to be partners with DirecTV was not as urgent. And not only that, but the new television services from Verizon and AT&T were meant to compete with DirecTV and EchoStar as well as the established cable giants.

The new wave of competition created problems for DirecTV. Profit margins in 2004 disappointed some investors, who felt the company was spending too heavily to gain new subscribers and not doing an effective enough job of holding on to existing ones. In the fourth quarter of 2005, the company reported that the number of new subscribers came in below Wall Street's expectations. Shares of DirecTV barely budged in 2004 and fell more than 15 percent in 2005. This was not what Murdoch had envisioned when he took control of the company.

Bill Jacobs, an analyst with Oakmark Funds, a large mutual fund family based in Chicago and owner of DirecTV shares, said in March 2006 that one way for DirecTV to do a better job facing the competitive challenges from the telecoms and cable companies was to try and restart talks with EchoStar about some sort of combination.

Jacobs argued that it might have gotten easier for DirecTV to buy EchoStar, since the advent of television service from Verizon and AT&T made it more difficult to argue that a combination of DirecTV and EchoStar would truly violate antitrust laws. He conceded that the history of bad blood between Murdoch and Ergen complicated the story but thought the two of them might be able to put their differences aside to focus on their common enemies in the telecom and cable businesses.

"Apparently, there is a much better relationship now between Murdoch and Ergen. Both look at broadband as a money pit. I think it does make sense for them to work together," Jacobs said. However, the two companies never engaged in any more serious talks about a merger or business alliance and both watched as the phone and cable companies continued to add more video subscribers.[18]

Murdoch would enjoy some solace in the fact that DirecTV's fortunes would turn around in 2006 thanks to a concerted effort to sign on higher-quality subscribers (by weeding out potential customers with poor credit histories). In addition, DirecTV's investment in high-definition satellites was starting to pay off, as the company was able to offer more HD channels than the cable and phone companies, a point not lost in DirecTV's marketing campaigns.

However, it was still too little too late for Murdoch. By late

2006, Murdoch was faced with a decision regarding DirecTV that he could not have expected to be faced with in 2003: either relinquish his stake of the U.S. satellite market or risk losing control of his entire company to Malone. The choice was obvious.

Back in January 2004, a mere month after News Corp. completed its acquisition of its stake in DirecTV, Malone made the first of several moves designed to show Murdoch that he wanted a bigger say in the decisions being made by News Corp.

On January 21, 2004, Malone's Liberty Media disclosed that it had acquired a 17 percent stake in the company and, of most interest to Murdoch, a 9.15 percent voting interest in News Corp. The company had bought 22 million shares with full voting rights and exchanged its limited-voting shares for voting shares to give it a total of 48 million voting shares. Liberty also owned another 210.8 million shares with limited voting power. As a result of this deal, Liberty was now News Corp.'s largest shareholder and it had amassed the second-largest voting stake behind the Murdoch family.

Liberty did not publicly express any dissatisfaction with News Corp. or Murdoch when announcing the new ownership stake. "We have capitalized on an opportunity to exchange nonvoting shares for voting shares at attractive prices to become the second-largest voting block in one of the world's premier media companies," said Liberty Media's president and CEO Robert Bennett in a statement, adding that "News Corp. is one of the few truly global media companies and we are very pleased we were able to leverage our substantial equity interest in News Corp. into a larger equity and voting stake."[19]

However, it was clear to media analysts that what Malone and Liberty were trying to do was force Murdoch into selling or swapping some of News Corp.'s assets that Malone coveted for his own media empire, namely DirecTV. In essence, Malone was signaling that he would be willing to sell back the voting interest he had amassed if News Corp. would surrender to him some of the properties he wanted for his own company.

Malone confirmed that this was in fact his strategy in an interview with the *Financial Times* in April 2004. "There are certain small assets that we feel fit Liberty better than News Corp.," Malone said in the interview. "We could exchange small amounts of our News Corp. shares back for these assets."[20]

This confrontation came at an awkward time for News Corp., since the company had just announced plans to reincorporate in the United States, a decision that Murdoch hoped would make it easier for the firm to access the capital markets in the United States as well as increase the company's attractiveness to potential U.S.-based money management firms. But by making this decision, Murdoch angered some in his native Australia, who viewed the company's reincorporation in the United States as a sign that Murdoch no longer felt Australia was an important market for the company.

So Murdoch had the unenviable task of both trying to assure longtime investors in Australia to not unload his stock and that he was not turning his back on them while also having to brace for what potentially could be a nasty fight with Malone regarding the future of the company.

Murdoch ultimately won approval from his shareholders to reincorporate in the United States on October 26, 2004. But on November 3, 2004, Malone fired the next salvo, announcing that Liberty Media planned to swap 84.7 million nonvoting shares of News Corp.'s shares with Merrill Lynch in exchange for News Corp. Class B shares with full voting power. That move, when completed, would give Malone a 17 percent voting interest in the company and would make it more difficult for Murdoch to assert full control over the firm.

The move apparently infuriated Murdoch and it did not take him long to take action. On November 8, 2004, just three days before the company's reincorporation in the United States was completed, News Corp. announced a stockholder rights plan, commonly known on Wall Street as a "poison pill."

Stockholder rights plans are designed to thwart unfriendly takeovers, and by instituting the plan Murdoch was clearly showing concern that Malone could make a run to acquire more of News Corp. in order to gain a controlling interest. As part of the News Corp. poison pill, the company said that if another entity sought to acquire more than a 15 percent stake in News Corp., existing shareholders would have the right to buy more stock at a discounted price. When a company floods the market with more shares in this way the hope is that it can prevent a takeover by another entity, since the would-be acquirer would suddenly be faced with a diluted ownership stake and would also have to pony up more cash to buy the newly minted shares.

In its release about the poison pill, News Corp. explicitly said the shareholder rights plan was a response to Malone's latest move. "On November 3, 2004, immediately after the Australian Federal Court approved the Company's reincorporation from Australia to Delaware, Liberty Media Corporation disclosed that it had entered into an arrangement with a third party allowing Liberty to acquire an additional 8 percent of News Corporation voting stock. This action was taken without any discussion with, or prior notice to, News Corporation. For this and other reasons the Company has put in place a Rights Plan to protect the best interests of all shareholders."[21]

Malone responded a month after this by disclosing that the swap with Merrill Lynch, originally scheduled to take place no later than April 2005, would now close in mid-January.

Following that move, little happened publicly between the two companies for nearly two years as Malone and Murdoch privately tried to negotiate an amicable way to end the standoff. In December 2006, News Corp. and Liberty finally reached an agreement, one that would effectively end Murdoch's quest to be as big a player in the U.S. satellite market as he was in Europe and Asia.

On December 22, News Corp. and Liberty Media announced that Liberty would exchange its entire investment in News Corp., which at the time represented a 16 percent stake, for News Corp.'s ownership interest in DirecTV—which had increased to 38 percent—three of Fox's regional sports networks and $550 million in cash.

News Corp. hailed the deal in a statement as something that would "unlock tremendous value" for shareholders, since the swap would immediately add to News Corp.'s earnings, would allow the company to sell DirecTV at an "attractive valuation on a tax-free basis" and would essentially amount to an $11 billion buyback of News Corp.'s stock.[22] Nowhere in the release was any mention made about Murdoch breathing a sigh of relief that Malone would no longer be a problem.

But in its own statement, Liberty Media attempted to take the high road and show that there were no hard feelings. "We are extremely pleased with the successful, tax-efficient conversion of our News holding. Our investment in DirecTV will create financial, operating, and strategic flexibility," said Malone. "Liberty's ownership of News has created tremendous value for our shareholders, and we are grateful to Rupert Murdoch and News management."[23]

Interestingly, when Murdoch spoke about the decision to sell the DirecTV stake at the McGraw-Hill media conference in February 2007, he sounded like a jilted lover, expressing disdain for a business and company that just three years earlier he had been touting as the most exciting aspect of the company's myriad businesses.

"The problem with satellite TV in the U.S. is that broadband via satellite can't deliver. There may eventually be a technology breakthrough but I don't think it will be WiMax," Murdoch said, referring to the ballyhooed wireless technology that some in the communications industry viewed as the best way to offer high-speed Internet access to the masses.[24]

Murdoch added that the challenges from the likes of AT&T, Verizon, Comcast and Time Warner were likely to increase. The telecoms were starting to add wireless phone service to their bundled package of offerings to consumers. And cable companies had partnered with telecom Sprint to add cell phone offerings to their stable of digital phone, video and Internet access.

"The appeal of triple play and potentially quadruple play with mobile from cable and phone companies is tough to compete with," Murdoch said. It was a rare admission of defeat from Murdoch. And it was probably long overdue, as media experts agreed that News Corp.'s move to get out of the U.S. satellite television business was a wise one.[25]

Shortly before DirecTV shareholders were set to vote on the News Corp.–Liberty Media swap in April 2007, Joseph Bonner, an analyst with Argus Research, said getting rid of DirecTV would be a boon for News Corp. shareholders, since it would let News Corp. exit the cutthroat U.S. satellite and cable TV market. But perhaps more importantly, the deal meant that Murdoch and other News Corp. executives no longer needed to worry about meddling from Malone.

"The Liberty-DirecTV deal removes an ongoing issue about what was going to happen with News Corp. stock and control of the company. That cloud has lifted. News Corp. can move forward and not have more of management's time devoted to this," Bonner said.[26]

The deal was stuck in regulatory limbo for more than a year, but after a thorough and lengthy review the Department of Justice and the Federal Communications Commission both allowed the deal to go through in the first quarter of 2008. On February 27, the exchange of Malone's stake in News Corp. for Murdoch's stake in DirecTV was at long last completed.

It was not yet completely certain what the swap with Liberty would do for Murdoch-controlled NDS Group—the technology supplier that counted DirecTV as its biggest customer. In February 2007, David Richardson, director of new media and business development liaison to the content industry for NDS, said that the transaction with Liberty Media should not have an effect on NDS's contract with DirecTV.[27]

Still, NDS's dependence on News Corp. could have become a problem with DirecTV no longer a part of the Murdoch empire and may be one reason it decided to go private in 2008. Richardson said that the company is steadily gaining new customers outside of the News Corp. family. He said one thing media companies like is that NDS is happy to be behind the scenes and let its customers use their own brand name, not NDS's, on set-top boxes, digital video recorders and other products.

"We're an infrastructure supplier. If there is one thing we are religious about, it's not to compete with our customers. TiVo failed with DirecTV because it didn't understand that," Richardson said.[28]

To that end, Richardson said NDS has been partnering with other media companies as well. It has developed interactive games based on cartoon characters from Viacom-owned Nickelodeon and also supplied technology to a Walt Disney–branded mobile digital media player. But Richardson conceded that having News Corp. as its top shareholder sometimes gets in the way of deals. "Attempts at partnerships sometimes run afoul," he said.[29]

And that's probably an apt way to sum up how Murdoch's wheeling and dealing, partnerships, mergers and acquisitions can sometimes run afoul. Although Murdoch failed in his efforts to be one of the leading players in the U.S. cable/satellite television distribution market, he was determined not to end up on the losing end of the stick in an area that had perhaps even greater potential than television: the Internet. Murdoch may have lost the battle for supremacy on the small screen, but he was not about to become an also-ran in the fight to control the personal computer, cell phone and other digital devices. Murdoch was about to become consumed by a new obsession.

CHAPTER 6

Rupert 2.0

Google's successful initial public offering in August 2004 caused a lot of lightbulbs to go off in the heads of both major media executives and investors.

Within a few months, Google, the world's top search engine, had a market value that exceeded News Corp.'s. And by mid-2005, Google's market capitalization would also surpass Walt Disney and Time Warner.

Google's reception on Wall Street was as clear a sign as any that the painful dot-com bust that companies endured in 2000, 2001 and 2002 was definitely over. Google's business model of selling advertising tied to keyword searches was proof positive that the Internet was a legitimate medium for advertisers.

Now the trick was for companies like News Corp. to play catch-up. Most media companies had a Web presence, but it was somewhat limited. Namely, media firms had Web sites for individual brands. Disney had ABC.com and ESPN.com, for example. Viacom had set up MTV.com and Nickelodeon.com. And News Corp. had Fox.com and Web sites for its newspapers as its main Internet beachhead.

But most major media companies had merely dipped their toes in the Internet waters because they were still wary of whether there was an actual business model in selling content and advertising online. What's more, the disastrous effects of the merger between AOL and Time Warner served as a not-so-subtle reminder of what could happen if an "old media" company drinks the Internet Kool-Aid and decides to transform itself into a "new media" firm.

Google changed all of this, though. Its success, as well as a resurgence from online portal Yahoo, raised the stakes for media firms. It was no longer an option to sit idly by and let Google, Yahoo and other Internet-only media companies reap all the benefits of the growing shift of advertising dollars from radio, television and print to the Web. Murdoch realized this and knew he had to act quickly.

"Two and a half years ago, it became suddenly apparent to me that in a booming economy, print and television advertising was not growing as fast as it had in the past," said Murdoch at McGraw-Hill's media conference in February 2007.[1]

Not surprisingly, News Corp. plunged into the online waters with a vengeance. By the summer of 2005, Murdoch had decided that News Corp. could not afford to watch new competitors steal business from him. So in July, Rupert found the religion that is the Internet and reinvented Fox and News Corp. in the process.

"Murdoch's gift is that he understands the entirety of the communications and media business," said Sir Martin Sorrell, chief executive officer of WPP Group, one of the world's largest advertising agencies and public relations firms, at a *Fortune* magazine–sponsored conference in Aspen, Colorado, in June 2006.[2]

"You can't be just a newspaper company. You can't be just a magazine company. It is all becoming blurred," Sorrell continued.[3]

On July 15, 2005, News Corp. announced that it was forming a new business unit called Fox Interactive Media, or FIM for short. The division was originally established to simply manage News Corp.'s in-house stable of Web properties, including Fox.com, Foxsports.com, Foxnews.com and the Web sites of individual local television stations owned by News Corp.

"We're launching this new unit after months of internal study and discussion among News Corp. senior management from all key divisions," said Murdoch at the time of the announcement. "Across the board, we believe no other media company has been as successful at creating distinctive content and finding ways to distribute it over every conceivable platform to mass audiences around the world. We're confident this success will translate to the Internet. We believe the time is right for the launch of FIM and we're committed to devoting the resources to make it one of the premier companies on the Web."[4]

But this was just a mere hint of much bigger things to come from News Corp. and Murdoch. A mere three days later, News Corp. surprised Wall Street by announcing it was spending $580 million to acquire the relatively unknown online media firm Intermix Media.

Intermix's major asset was a social networking site called MySpace that was started just two years earlier. Social networking was just starting to become a big buzzword in online media circles and MySpace had quickly emerged as the top Web destination for young (translation: desirable to advertisers) Web users to go to hang out and chat with their friends.

MySpace had also gained a reputation for being a site that helped established musical artists like R.E.M. and Nine Inch Nails promote their albums to a younger audience as well as a place where unsigned bands could try and make a name for themselves.

Murdoch instantly realized that MySpace, in addition to being a potential gold mine for online advertising dollars, also could serve an important role as a means for News Corp. to promote its TV shows, movies and books to a demographic it may not easily be able to reach otherwise.

"Intermix's brands, such as MySpace.com, are some of the Web's hottest properties and resonate with the same audiences that are most attracted to Fox's news, sports and entertainment offerings. We see a great opportunity to combine the popularity of Intermix's sites, particularly MySpace, with our existing on-line assets to provide a richer experience for today's Internet users," Murdoch said at the time of the Intermix acquisition.[5]

This was only the beginning of what would turn out to be a veritable cyber–shopping spree for Murdoch. Two weeks after announcing the Intermix purchase, News Corp. said that FIM was buying Scout Media, which owned online sports network Scout.com, a site formed in 2001 with the financial backing of former NFL quarterback Bernie Kosar.

Scout.com focused on player news for high school, college and professional sports and was therefore a good Internet companion to News Corp.'s regional cable sports television and radio programming. News Corp. did not say at the time how much it paid for Scout Media, but it was later disclosed in a regulatory filing that the purchase price was $60 million.

During the company's fiscal fourth-quarter 2005 earnings conference call with analysts in August 2005, Murdoch hinted that the company was not yet done buying online properties either.

"There is no greater priority for the company today than to meaningfully and profitably expand its Internet presence and to properly position ourselves to benefit from the explosion in broadband usage that we are now starting to see," he said.[6]

And a little more than a month after the Scout deal was announced, Murdoch was at it again. This time, News Corp. set its sight on the lucrative video game market, agreeing to buy IGN Entertainment on September 8, 2005, for $650 million.

IGN owned several popular Web sites focusing on the gaming community, including GameSpy, TeamXbox, 3D Gamers and GameStats.com. The company also owned movie review and preview site Rotten Tomatoes as well as AskMen.com, a lifestyle guide that was kind of an online equivalent of men's magazines *GQ* and *Maxim*.

In a period of just three months, News Corp. spent nearly $1.3 billion to go from being a nominal player in the online media space to one of the largest Web properties. Murdoch was obviously pleased with his new Internet toys.

"We have gone a long way toward achieving two of our key strategic objectives in our efforts to become a leading and profitable Internet presence. First, we have significantly enhanced our online reach," Murdoch proudly proclaimed following the IGN deal.

"Second, we have furthered our strategy to leverage the unique competencies the company enjoys with its news, sports, and entertainment assets to create a leading Internet destination. By acquiring IGN and its compelling sites, we now have top entertainment sites to go along with FOXSports.com, as well as our myriad news sites," Murdoch added.[7]

Although some media analysts have scoffed at how much money Murdoch had to spend to build his nascent Web empire, others argued that News Corp. was able to go from being an "old media" laggard to one of the most aggressive major media companies online and that $1.3 billion was not too significant a price to accomplish this transition.

"There are likely to be only a few winners in social networking and user-generated content. MySpace was a steal for Rupert Murdoch," said Andrew Metrick, a professor of finance at the Wharton School at the University of Pennsylvania who specializes in the subject of venture capital investing.[8]

Murdoch further described his newfound obsession with the Internet during his speech to shareholders at the company's annual meeting in 2005. "Empowering the consumer through greater choice is exactly what this Company strives to accomplish. And there's no greater medium of choice than the Internet. That's why we are so drawn to the opportunities and challenges it represents. This is a time of fundamental change. So with relatively modest and extremely well-targeted investments, we have this year formed a special Internet unit and acquired properties that have instantly delivered us tens of millions of new customers, and, in the process, begun a transformation of the Company," he said, adding that "we have now the most potent combination of relevant content and critical audience mass to forge a real and profitable presence on the Web."[9]

And News Corp. was not done buying digital media assets. In September 2006, the company announced it was spending $188 million to buy a controlling stake in Jamba!, a leading provider of games, ring tones, music and other entertainment for cell phones and other mobile devices, from technology company VeriSign. News Corp. merged Jamba! with its own Fox Mobile Entertainment unit.

In May 2007, FIM acquired both Photobucket and Flektor, two popular sites used to create, store and share online photo slide shows and videos. News Corp. followed up those deals with the purchase of Beliefnet, an online community dedicated to news about various faiths, religions and spirituality, in December 2007.

Many on Wall Street believe News Corp. is not finished assembling the pieces of its Web strategy, with several analysts speculating that News Corp. could one day make a bid for LinkedIn, a privately held company that runs a site that allows businesspeople to network and share contacts (it's invariably described as a "MySpace for grown-ups"), as well as for Monster Worldwide, the publicly traded firm that owns online career site Monster.com. The company has denied being interested in either firm, however.

Some analysts give Murdoch and other News Corp. executives credit for not tinkering too much with MySpace and giving the site's chief executive officer and cofounder Chris DeWolfe the flexibility to run the site pretty much in the same fashion as when owned by Intermix.

"News Corp. and Fox recognize the importance of allowing people to be alone with their friends so they do not feel like they are being looked at by Big Brother," says Emily Riley, an analyst with Jupiter Research who follows social networking sites. "They understand how many competitors they have nipping at their heels right now, so they are doing everything they can not to alienate their users."[10]

To that end, DeWolfe said at *Fortune*'s Brainstorm conference in June 2006 that the key to MySpace's continued success was not to make it look like the site's decision making was now being dictated by Murdoch's whims.

"Everything we've done since beginning MySpace has always been a function of just what users asked us for. If we stay true to what our users want and position changes in a proper way we will be all right," DeWolfe said.[11]

Of course, it's not as if MySpace has been completely free of News Corp.'s influence. DeWolfe admitted that MySpace was being used to some extent, as Murdoch originally envisioned when buying Intermix, as a way to plug Fox content.

"There is a fair amount of synergy. When people think of News Corp. they may think of the Fox channel and Fox News first," DeWolfe said. "So there is a lot of crossover and potential for interesting promotions."[12]

MySpace has grown even more under News Corp. ownership, as have other online properties Murdoch has acquired. The site now operates in more than twenty countries, having entered Japan and China since 2006. In February 2007 at McGraw-Hill's media conference, Murdoch said that the increase in users and traffic was faster than expected and suggested that "we almost had to put the brakes" on growth, particularly in international markets.

"Advertising sales have gone from basically nothing to about $25 million a month," he said.[13]

During an earnings conference call in August 2007, Murdoch

told investors that he expected News Corp.'s Fox Interactive Media unit, which includes MySpace, to post annual revenue of more than $1 billion in 2008 and generate operating profit margins in excess of 20 percent.[14]

What's more, Murdoch said that within the next three to five years, he believed Fox Interactive Media could generate over 10 percent of News Corp.'s overall sales and be the company's biggest driver of profit growth. To put that in perspective, analysts expect News Corp. to post annual sales of $36.8 billion in the fiscal year that ends in June 2010. So in order for Murdoch's prediction about FIM's sales to come true, revenue would need to nearly quadruple from the $1 billion expected in 2008 to almost $3.7 billion by 2010.[15]

That may not be a reasonable estimate. A big question dogging News Corp. and Murdoch since buying MySpace is whether MySpace or any of the other online assets News Corp. has folded into FIM will really ever generate the billions of dollars in sales and profits needed to justify the price paid for them.

A big part of MySpace's revenue stream, though, comes from a partnership that MySpace announced in conjunction with Google in August 2006. As part of that deal, Google became the exclusive provider of search and keyword advertising on MySpace and most other FIM properties.

The deal called for minimum revenue-sharing payments of $900 million for News Corp. from the first quarter of 2007 through the second quarter of 2010. This agreement was widely viewed as a major victory for News Corp., proof that MySpace was more than just a cool Web site for twentysomething slackers; it was also a bona fide generator of revenue and profits. During a News Corp. earnings conference call in February 2007, Murdoch said he would be "shocked" if most of the money from Google did not flow to MySpace's and News Corp.'s bottom line.

Analysts were pleased by this development and hailed News Corp. and Murdoch for showing that MySpace had a legitimate business model. "Now that Google's ad sharing revenue relationship is starting to kick in with MySpace, that partnership should work fine. Growth from MySpace is intact," said David Joyce, an analyst who covers News Corp. for Wall Street firm Miller Tabak + Company.[16]

But shortly after the first payments from Google started to be made to News Corp., there were rumblings that Google had already grown dissatisfied with the arrangement, since apparently social networking sites like MySpace are not generating as much advertising revenue for Google as the company had originally hoped for.

In a conference call with analysts and investors in January 2008, Google cofounder Sergey Brin, when discussing why the company's fourth-quarter 2007 earnings missed Wall Street's forecasts, cited poor advertising performance from its social networking partners as a primary reason.

At first Brin only admitted to a "challenge" with its social networking inventory and that the company did not want to "talk about individual partners' performance or anything like that."[17] But when pressed to talk in more detail about why social networking advertising was not yet panning out, Brin did name MySpace as one of its largest social networking partners. He also sounded more guarded about whether advertising revenue from social networking sites would truly be a big market for Google.

"I don't think we have the killer best way to advertise and monetize the social networks yet. We're running lots of experiments. We had some significant improvements but as I said, some of the things we were working on in the fourth quarter didn't really pan out and there were some disappointments there. I hope to be able to report more progress in the future," Brin said.[18]

Murdoch and Chernin countered during a News Corp. earnings conference call in February 2008 that they were not concerned. Murdoch maintained that News Corp. had "invested smartly in social networking," while Chernin said that MySpace was gaining momentum with advertisers.[19]

And at a Bear Stearns media conference in March 2008, Murdoch continued to tout the promise of MySpace and the relationship with Google. He said that MySpace could wind up being "another form of real targeted advertising" for News Corp. As for Google, Murdoch simply said that "we're very happy to be in the Google camp. They do our search advertising and pay us well for it."[20]

However, despite Murdoch's glowing comments, it remained uncertain how long MySpace's momentum with advertisers would last. In addition to the problems Google had monetizing MySpace's traffic in the early stages of its deal with FIM, News Corp. also needed to be concerned with the possibility that MySpace's popularity may have already peaked.

Although MySpace's traffic had grown dramatically since News Corp. acquired Intermix in 2005, figures from Web research firm comScore show that page views and unique visitors in early 2008 were lower than the levels of just a few months earlier, an alarming sign for a site and business that was supposed to be still in its early stages of explosive growth.

MySpace's January 2008 unique visitor count of 68.6 million was down nearly 5 percent from the all-time high of about 72 million in October 2007. What's more, MySpace's page views in January 2008 stood at 43.3 billion, down 7 percent from the peak of 46.5 billion page views in the United States in June 2007.

And the sluggish start to the Google-MySpace ad-sharing arrangement added to growing tensions between Google and News Corp. In March 2007, News Corp. announced that it was joining forces with GE's NBC Universal unit to form an online video joint venture. The site, later dubbed Hulu, was referred to by many online media experts as a direct shot at Google and its popular online video subsidiary YouTube, which Google had acquired for nearly $1.7 billion in October 2006.

YouTube, which was founded in February 2005, quickly

incurred the wrath of several traditional media companies because many YouTube users had uploaded copyrighted programming to the Web site. One media giant, Viacom, decided that the best way to get Google and YouTube to do a better job of policing the site for pirated content was to take them to court.

Viacom announced in March 2007 that it was suing Google and YouTube for copyright infringement and was demanding $1 billon in damages. As of July 2008, the lawsuit was still pending. But News Corp. did not join in the lawsuit. Instead it decided to partner with NBC to create what the financial press often referred to as a "YouTube killer."

Even before the launch of Hulu, Murdoch was doing his best to talk down the significance of YouTube's threat to News Corp. At a Goldman Sachs media conference in September 2006, a month before Google bought YouTube, Murdoch said he thought that MySpace Videos would soon take the online video market share lead from YouTube.

But in February 2007, he boasted about how MySpace's video site was "clearly number two" to YouTube. However, he also said that "if you look carefully" at YouTube, it "is not much of a community site" and added that while it could be a "quite hypnotic" experience it was not really a true threat to the economics of television or to MySpace, for that matter.[21]

This may be just wishful thinking, however, as a look at some of the traffic figures for MySpace and YouTube clearly show that YouTube is in many respects eclipsing MySpace in terms of popularity.

According to figures from comScore, 3.3 billion videos were viewed at Google-owned video sites (and more than 97 percent of that total came from YouTube) in December 2007, far outpacing the number of videos watched at MySpace and other Fox Interactive Media sites. Only 358.4 million videos were viewed at FIM sites in December 2007. Google's market share was 32.6 percent compared to just 3.5 percent for FIM.

For Murdoch, this was not something he could have expected when he bought MySpace. YouTube, after all, was only a couple of months old and few were talking about the concept of online video sharing becoming a major business, particularly the kind of user-generated videos that were popular on YouTube. To that end, when Murdoch announced the acquisition of Intermix in July 2005, the word "video" was mentioned only once in the press release, compared to six references to the concept of "social networking."

What's more, Murdoch and News Corp. were usually the upstarts that came into an established industry, shook it up and eventually emerged victorious. So he was in the uncomfortable position of playing catch-up in a new industry that he thought he had already essentially sealed up. Murdoch was also used to having the luxury of years, if not decades, for a business venture to prove itself. Neither Fox nor Fox Business were immediate successes. But the Internet has turned out to be a much different arena than television. New sites can quickly sprout up and flourish, even without the backing of a major media company like News Corp.

In addition, it appeared that Murdoch also had to worry as much about staying ahead of Yahoo, Viacom, Microsoft, Time Warner and Disney as he did about catching up to Google and YouTube. Yahoo, for example, had a 3.4 percent share of the online video market, just a tad behind FIM. And the other four companies had market shares between 1.2 percent and 2.3 percent.

Perhaps more worrisome to Murdoch had to be the fact that, according to figures from Nielsen//NetRatings, another company that tracks Web traffic, YouTube had slightly more unique viewers in the United States in January 2008 than all of Fox Interactive Media's sites combined.

Murdoch's downplaying of YouTube as a legitimate rival could simply be a sign that he realizes the explosive growth potential for MySpace may be short-lived. In other words, if Murdoch can't be number one in a category, he'll try and dismiss the importance of it so that maybe people will ignore the fact that News Corp. isn't in the lead. "We believe the way to keep advertising is to be number one in everything we do," he said at the Bear Stearns conference in March 2008.[22]

In the world of the Web, young, attention-deficit consumers have a way of quickly latching on to the next big thing. MySpace, after all, was viewed by many simply as the social networking fad that bumped off the once-popular Friendster as the biggest social networking site on the Web. But in 2007, MySpace increasingly found that Google and Yahoo may not be its biggest threats. The worry was that MySpace was starting to lose buzz to the latest kid on the social networking block—Facebook.

"For some number of users, MySpace is already passé. There is a fickle dimension to these audiences," says Greg Sterling, principal with Sterling Market Intelligence, an independent research firm based in Oakland, California, that specializes in analyzing online advertising trends.[23]

Facebook began as a social networking site popular mainly with college kids. The company was founded by wunderkind Mark Zuckerberg in his Harvard dorm room when he was just twenty years old. But Facebook rapidly took on a life of its own and became a major competitor to MySpace beyond college campuses.

In addition, Facebook's popularity and Web traffic grew exponentially beginning in May 2007 when the company announced that it was letting outside developers build their own Web applications that can run within Facebook. MySpace, at the time, did not have its own program for developers. It did not announce its own open platform for developers until October 2007. So again, not unlike with YouTube, Murdoch was in the uncomfortable position of having to follow the creative new hotshots instead of blazing his own trail.

As a result, Facebook started getting more and more attention from both the technology press in Silicon Valley and Wall Street. Microsoft and Google were said to be engaged in a bidding war for a piece of Facebook. Microsoft ultimately won the battle and agreed to pay $240 million in October 2007 for a 1.6 percent stake in Facebook. That investment meant Facebook was being valued at $15 billion, more than what most analysts on Wall Street felt MySpace—and all of Fox Interactive Media, for that matter—was worth.

And as Facebook's popularity grew, News Corp. became more defensive regarding Facebook. Murdoch doesn't like coming in second. At the McGraw-Hill conference in February 2007, Murdoch tried to downplay the growing threat of Facebook by saying that the social networking market was not a zero-sum game, that there was room for both MySpace and Facebook, as teens and young adults were unlikely to completely abandon profile pages on one social networking site and uproot to a new site.

"A lot of young people and college kids are undoubtedly going to Facebook. But that doesn't mean they don't also stay with MySpace," Murdoch said.[24]

But in July 2007, just as chatter was beginning to build that Facebook could be worth somewhere between $5 billion and $10 billion, News Corp. issued a press release that served as nothing more than a reminder that MySpace was still bigger than Facebook.

The release stated, without ever mentioning Facebook by name, that MySpace attracted more users than its "closest competitor in the social networking category" and that MySpace users also visited the site more often and spent more time at the site than did users of other social networking sites.

Murdoch himself grew much testier when asked about the upstart site. During a Goldman Sachs media conference in September 2007, he responded to one analyst's question about Facebook by reciting what the latest online page view numbers for the site were at the time and declaring that "Facebook is infinitely smaller than MySpace."[25]

Murdoch went on to attack what he perceived as Facebook's lax standards regarding safety for Facebook's users. He quipped that "if you wanted to stalk a young girl on Facebook, it would be very very easy. You can't do that on MySpace."[26]

Those comments took many in the industry by surprise, since at the time MySpace, along with Facebook, was the target of criticism from many state attorneys general in 2007 due to news reports of adults using the social networking site to prey on young children.

While the site was fairly proactive in taking steps to ensure that inappropriate behavior and sexual predators were quickly removed from the site, MySpace and government authorities did have a rocky period before agreeing to work closely together. MySpace was involved in a brief legal spat with eight states in May 2007 regarding information about users who were registered sex offenders.

MySpace initially refused to hand over to the eight states the names and other details about seven thousand users whose profile pages had been deleted by MySpace because of their criminal records. The company argued that since the states only requested the information in a letter as opposed to with a subpoena, it was not legally obligated to give the states the data. Following public outcries from several of the attorneys general and ongoing negotiations, MySpace ultimately agreed to the request.

MySpace quickly moved to bolster the security for its users after that, removing more than twenty-nine thousand registered sex offenders from the site. Still, it wasn't until January 2008 that MySpace announced a comprehensive plan to cooperate with states regarding the safety of its users. As part of the announcement, MySpace pledged to make the pages of all sixteen- and seventeen-year-old users private—the previous default was to have only the pages of fourteen- and fifteen-year-olds private—and also agreed to work on creating a registry of children's e-mail addresses that would let parents block their kids from using those addresses to establish profile pages on MySpace or other social networking sites.

The plan was lauded by state attorneys general as well as child activist groups. But it is more than a bit curious that Murdoch would lash out at Facebook for its safety problems while at the same time MySpace was dealing with the issues and was just starting to address them in a significant way.

The criticism appeared to be nothing more than a prime example of Murdoch attacking a competitor when he feels threatened. For someone who claimed that he was not that concerned about Facebook, he talked an awful lot about it. Wall Street recognized this and some analysts said fears that MySpace's popularity had peaked and that Facebook would do to MySpace what

MySpace did to Friendster. This was beginning to take its toll on the stock price.

There was no denying that Facebook had stolen some of MySpace's thunder. According to figures from comScore, Facebook's average monthly unique visitors in the United States surged 47 percent between April 2007 and January 2008, from 23 million to 33.9 million. MySpace's unique visitors rose just 3 percent during the same time frame, from 66.8 million to 68.7 million.

"The growth trajectory is still tremendous for MySpace. But part of the chatter behind News Corp.'s stock lagging is concern about MySpace's traction versus Facebook," said David Bank, an analyst with RBC Capital Markets.[27]

With all this in mind, there were talks in early 2008 that News Corp. might seek to abandon the Google ad-sharing deal with MySpace in favor of a new deal with Microsoft. What's more, News Corp. was also said to have restarted discussions that it originally began having with Google's top rival Yahoo in the summer of 2007 about combining the operations of FIM and Yahoo into one company that News Corp. would own a minority stake in.

But Murdoch has repeatedly and adamantly said that he is interested neither in bidding for all of Yahoo nor in spinning off his interest in MySpace and Fox Interactive Media into a separate company. "There is no attraction at this time," Murdoch said during News Corp.'s earnings conference call in August 2006 when asked if he would be interested in buying

Yahoo, adding that he thought News Corp. would be able to build FIM into an online media powerhouse to rival Yahoo and Google, "given time."[28] Murdoch reiterated these comments in February 2008. "We are definitely not going to make a bid for Yahoo. We are not interested at this stage."[29] Murdoch added a month later at the Bear Stearns conference that "we're not going to get into a fight with Microsoft, which has a lot more money than us."[30] Murdoch was referring to Microsoft's $44.6 billion takeover bid for Yahoo. Microsoft made that offer to Yahoo in January 2008. Yahoo rejected it and wound up turning down another offer from Microsoft in May 2008 for $47.5 billion.

Ultimately, Microsoft dropped its bid for Yahoo. And talks between News Corp. and Yahoo about a joint venture fell apart because Murdoch and Yahoo could not agree on a fair price for MySpace. News Corp. reportedly wanted to own a 20 percent stake in a combined FIM-Yahoo entity. Murdoch insisted that, at a bare minimum, Yahoo should value MySpace at $6 billion in a merger. Some Internet analysts suggested that Murdoch wanted a valuation as high as $10 billion.

Interestingly, Murdoch also downplayed the thought of News Corp. making many more acquisitions in the Internet medium, partly because of concerns about companies being too expensive. "We're constantly looking at things and venture capitalists bring us stuff at stupid prices," he said. "People open their mouths and talk about how they just want a billion dollars because it will be soon that they will be breaking even. Sometimes we're cautious, a little too cautious. But it would be very easy to throw away a lot of money buying Internet sites that will not fulfill their promise."[31]

It was a stunning admission from someone who has never really considered price to be a major stumbling block to getting what he wants. It's particularly astonishing considering that the comments came less than three years after Murdoch was spending billions on Internet companies and waxing rhapsodic about their potential.

But as Murdoch quickly learned, staying on top of the online media world is not easy. It is a business subject to the demands of users who are less loyal to brand names in media than the typical television watcher or moviegoer. As a result, more acquisitions, and perhaps a major one, may be necessary to keep other competitors at bay. So Murdoch may have also been merely trying to talk down the potential price he would have to pay for other online firms.

For what it's worth, Murdoch has talked often in the past about not being interested in buying a company, only to go out and eventually make a bid for it later. There is no better example of that than Murdoch's quest to take over Dow Jones, a deal that not only will further News Corp.'s position in the newspaper business, but will also become one of the more important linchpins in the company's overall digital media strategy.

CHAPTER 7

The Battle for Dow Jones

When News Corp. stunned Wall Street by announcing on May 1, 2007, that it was offering to buy the venerable publisher of the *Wall Street Journal* for $5 billion, the only thing that really should have surprised Murdoch watchers was that he hadn't made the offer sooner.

Dow Jones had been struggling, along with the rest of the newspaper industry, to effectively transition to the digital world. Readers and advertisers were increasingly migrating from print publications to the Web. Some of the negativity surrounding newspaper publishers on Wall Street was probably a bit overblown. Print isn't likely to die, as some assert. But the financial woes facing newspaper publishers like Dow Jones made it obvious that some kind of shakeup in the industry was needed.

In June 2005, British media columnist Peter Preston wrote in a column in the *Observer* that Dow Jones was vulnerable to a takeover. "A daily paper distributed in so many cities around the world cannot always make the sheer weight of numbers of its American base count in ad agency eyes—and any daily in that position is going to find added difficulties when readership drains on to the Internet," Preston wrote, adding that Murdoch would be an obvious buyer.[1]

To a large degree, consolidation in newspapers had already begun. Lee Enterprises bought Pulitzer Inc. for nearly $1.5 billion in 2005. Knight Ridder, which had resisted shareholders' calls to sell for years, finally relented in March 2006, when it agreed to be purchased by rival McClatchy Company for $4.5 billion. And In April 2007, Tribune Company, which publishes well-known papers such as its flagship *Chicago Tribune*, the *Los Angeles Times* and, at the time, the Long Island paper *Newsday*, announced it was being acquired by real estate mogul Sam Zell for $8.2 billion and would be taken private.

And it was no secret that Murdoch, despite Wall Street's bearish stance on the newspaper industry, had not lost his love for the business that News Corp. had its roots in.

In fact, some thought in early 2007 that if Murdoch were to make a newspaper deal, the likeliest one would either have been a play for *Tribune* or, at the very least, a purchase of *Newsday* from Tribune. Combining *Newsday*'s operations with the *New York Post*'s could have generated large cost savings for News Corp.

The *New York Post*, in addition to being famous for its salacious headlines, is also well-known in media circles for its perennial struggles to garner a big profit for News Corp. "If we could pull off a *Newsday* deal, the *Post* would have a viable business model within five minutes," Murdoch said in February 2007 at the McGraw-Hill media conference.[2]

And Murdoch eventually did try to pull off a *Newsday* deal. In the spring of 2008, he offered to pay Zell, the *Tribune's* new owner, $580 million for the publication. But New York–based cable company Cablevision outbid Murdoch, offering $630 million for *Newsday*. In a rare show of fiscal restraint, Murdoch decided to resist a bidding war with Cablevision and wound up withdrawing his offer.

Losing *Newsday* was a blow to Murdoch. But the motivation behind buying that paper was purely financial. A purchase of *Newsday* would not have given Murdoch what he's craved for decades: one of the most widely respected brands in the news world. Before his bid for Dow Jones, Murdoch's name was associated with sensational, gossip-laden tabloids and a partisan television network.

Owning Dow Jones, specifically the *Wall Street Journal*, would instantly give Murdoch that journalistic credibility he so desperately wanted—even though he knew that skeptics would come out of the woodwork to speculate on how quickly Murdoch would tarnish the good name of Dow Jones.

But first Murdoch had to convince the Bancroft family to sell to him. That would not be easy. The Bancrofts were reluctant to give up control of a company that their family had controlled since 1902.

The Bancrofts, through a Byzantine series of trusts, owned 64 percent of the voting shares of Dow Jones. So it would have been impossible for Murdoch to win control of Dow Jones without the backing of the Bancrofts. Making matters more complex, there were nearly three dozen members of the Bancroft family, each with different opinions about the sale of the company.

In fact, Murdoch's wooing of the Bancrofts was an exercise that was more than a decade in the making. In a column written for Britain's *Evening Standard* in August 2004, David Yelland, who had been the editor of Murdoch's *Sun* from 1998 to 2003 and prior to that was business editor of the *New York Post*, suggested that Murdoch had made his first attempt to buy Dow Jones during the 1990s.

"Back in the 1990s, when I was business editor of Murdoch's *New York Post* way before he brought me home to edit the *Sun*, Rupert came reasonably close to securing the support of some of the disparate families who control the *Wall Street Journal's* parent company, Dow Jones," Yelland wrote.[3]

At the time this article was written, Yelland argued that it was more likely Murdoch would try to buy the *Financial Times* from British media company Pearson. In fact, Yelland wrote that he believed Murdoch would "move heaven and earth" to get the *FT*.[4]

Yelland would turn out to be wrong about Murdoch's target, but he was spot-on regarding Murdoch's desire to do whatever it takes to acquire Dow Jones.

News Corp.'s $5 billion bid for Dow Jones valued the company at $60 a share. Not only was that a 65 percent premium over what the stock was trading the day before the offer was announced, it was also a price that Dow Jones shares had not traded at since April 2002. That reality was a stunning confirmation of just how bad the business environment was for newspaper publishers. Because of the declines in circulation and advertising sales for many publishers, Wall Street soured on the prospects of newspaper companies. As a result, some analysts thought the Bancrofts should rush to take the $60 a share offer. Many media observers felt the stock would never reach that level again if the company remained independent.

On the surface, the decision to sell should have been a no-brainer. Dow Jones had been a huge disappointment for investors for the past five years. But this offer was not enough to immediately convince the Bancrofts that selling to Murdoch, a man so demonized that Jack Shafer, editor at large of online publication *Slate*, continuously has referred to him as an "old rotten bastard," was the right thing to do.

The news of the offer quickly sparked reports that other companies would come in with a counterbid for Dow Jones. And Murdoch, true to form, quickly went on the attack to defend the offer.

During News Corp.'s fiscal third quarter 2007 earnings conference call on May 9, 2007—just eight days after News Corp. announced its bid for Dow Jones—Murdoch said that Dow Jones had "a great collection of assets" but maintained that Dow Jones was "a company with limited resources."[5]

Murdoch also made it clear that the $60-a-share offer for

Dow Jones would be the only one. He was not interested in negotiating a deal in the event that the Bancrofts were holding out for more money. In other words, he was willing to walk away if the Bancrofts could not agree to a sale.

"We would not have made this generous offer if we did not have confidence in our company. We made an offer at what we feel is a more than full and fair price," Murdoch said.[6]

Nonetheless, opposition to the deal was immense. Several members of the Bancroft family expressed reluctance to sell to Murdoch due to fears about what would happen to the editorial integrity and independence at the *Journal* and other Dow Jones publications.

That sentiment was echoed by the IAPE, the union representing more than 2000 Dow Jones workers. The day the bid for Dow Jones was announced, the IAPE issued a harshly worded statement urging the Bancrofts to reject the deal.

"The staff, from top to bottom, opposes a Rupert Murdoch takeover of Dow Jones & Co. Since the early part of the twentieth century, the Bancroft family has stood up for the independence and quality of the *Wall Street Journal* and has built it into one of the world's great newspapers. Mr. Murdoch has shown a willingness to crush quality and independence, and there is no reason to think he would handle Dow Jones or the *Journal* any differently," the IAPE said.[7]

But the cold, harsh reality of the situation was that Murdoch had put Dow Jones in play, plain and simple. Shares of Dow Jones surged more than 57 percent the day the offer was announced, which meant that Wall Street was clearly betting that the company would eventually agree to a sale around the $60 price that Murdoch was offering.

There was no turning back for the Bancrofts and the board of Dow Jones. It was one thing to say no to Murdoch, but large institutional shareholders of the company would have revolted if the Bancrofts decided to remain independent. Their options were either to accept Murdoch's bid or find a so-called white knight suitor to make an attractive counteroffer to News Corp.'s deal.

Going private was not really a viable option for the company, since the credit markets were beginning to collapse in the spring of 2007 due to the subprime mortgage crisis. Private equity firms would have had a tough time raising the necessary cash to finance a $5 billion-plus deal for Dow Jones.

In addition, many private equity firms simply didn't have any interest in bidding for a slow-growth company like Dow Jones, especially at a 65 percent premium. And Murdoch knew this.

"The economics for anyone else doing this deal but News Corp. makes it very difficult. Sure, the union is desperate and everyone is afraid of Murdoch. But anyone who is a serious player who wants to make some money from Dow Jones is going to be hard-pressed to pay $60 for it," said Edward Atorino, an analyst who follows the newspaper industry for research firm Benchmark Company, shortly after the bid was announced.[8]

Nonetheless, the IAPE hired an adviser in June 2007 to help it find other buyers. And names did surface. There were reports that billionaire supermarket mogul Ron Burkle was interested in making an offer. *Philadelphia Inquirer* owner Brian Tierney said he would be interested in a deal if he could find other partners.

Brad Greenspan, a Web entrepreneur, made a formal offer to buy 25 percent of Dow Jones for $60 a share. He claimed that such a deal would give Dow Jones the necessary cash to keep it growing but also to allow the Bancrofts to retain control of the company. Ironically, Greenspan was a cofounder of MySpace. But he had left Intermix Media before it was sold to News Corp.

However, investors did not feel that any of these possible suitors would emerge as serious bidders for Dow Jones. But there were large corporations that gave the deal serious thought. Those companies were motivated by a strong desire to keep News Corp. and Rupert Murdoch from acquiring the preeminent source of financial news.

First and foremost, General Electric was viewed as the company that stood to lose the most if Dow Jones fell into Murdoch's clutches. While GE's CNBC network had a contract to share news-gathering sources with the *Journal* that lasted until 2011, some feared that if Murdoch acquired Dow Jones he would look to restructure that arrangement.

At the very least, many media experts felt that buying Dow Jones might be a wise defensive move for General Electric. It would prevent Murdoch from gaining the type of credibility in the financial journalism world that he could use to build buzz for his upcoming Fox Business Network (which would have to go head-to-head with GE's CNBC financial network).

"For Murdoch, this is an opportunity to develop an even greater worldwide brand. It just makes perfect sense," said Larry Grimes, president of W. B. Grimes, an investment bank based in Gaithersburg, Maryland, that focuses on media mergers, on the day the Dow Jones bid was announced.[9] To that end, Barry Ritholtz, director of equity research for Fusion IQ, an asset management firm based in New York, said that GE should have bought Dow Jones simply to keep it away from News Corp.

In addition, Ritholtz said that combining Dow Jones with the rest of GE's NBC Universal media properties could have been an elegant solution to a problem facing GE, namely pressure from analysts and institutional investors to dump the struggling media division. "If GE bought Dow Jones, they could then spin out their entire media group as NBC Universal at a higher valuation than what it's currently worth," Ritholtz said, adding that he did not understand why GE wouldn't launch its own bid for Dow Jones without seeking other backers.[10]

"I can't explain why GE needs a partner. This would be a rounding error for them. GE wants to protect CNBC, and it would be intriguing for them to take all their media properties and make it a standalone company," he said.[11]

But it wasn't that simple. GE, despite its pristine balance

sheet, seemed unwilling to pony up $5 billion of its own money just to play defense. After all, a deal for Dow Jones would undoubtedly be dilutive to earnings in the short term, given how high the premium would have to be for GE to top the Murdoch offer.

How badly did Murdoch want Dow Jones? Consider this: At the time the deal was announced, search engine Google was trading at thirty-one times 2007 earnings forecasts. While not cheap, this valuation was considered reasonable by many investors, since Wall Street analysts were predicting that Google's profits would grow at a 30 percent rate annually for the next few years. Google, after all, was the market leader in online search advertising, one of the most rapidly growing areas of the media business. Dow Jones, on the other hand, was a stodgy newspaper publisher. And even though Dow Jones was expanding online, it still was wedded to the dying print business and could not hope to match Google's growth potential.

But Murdoch's $60 bid for Dow Jones valued Dow Jones at nearly forty times 2007 earnings estimates, a staggering price to pay for a company whose earnings were expected to increase at just a 13 percent clip annually, on average, for the next few years, according to Wall Street analysts.

Murdoch hoped that his "generous" bid would scare away other interested parties. However, GE and others did consider their own offers for Dow Jones. GE first turned to Microsoft about teaming up on a bid for Dow Jones. A month after News Corp. announced its bid, GE and Microsoft held exploratory talks about matching Murdoch's offer. But Microsoft quickly walked away.

Next, GE approached Pearson, a company once partially owned by Murdoch (he held a 20 percent interest in the company in the late 1980s and sold his stake at the height of News Corp.'s financial crisis). Pearson, unlike Microsoft, was interested. The British media firm also had a compelling reason to keep Dow Jones from Murdoch, since the *Wall Street Journal* was a top competitor with both Pearson's *Financial Times* and the *Economist*, a weekly business magazine in which Pearson held a 50 percent stake.

According to reports in both the *Financial Times* and the *Wall Street Journal*, Pearson and GE even considered structuring a deal for Dow Jones so that the Bancrofts could keep a 20 percent stake in the combined company.

The thought was that a merger of GE's CNBC, Pearson's *Financial Times* and the *Economist* with the *Wall Street Journal*, Dow Jones Newswires, weekly magazine *Barron's* and the Web site MarketWatch would be an unrivaled leader in the financial news world. Such a combination would make it difficult for Murdoch's new cable business channel to compete effectively with CNBC. It would have been very tough, if not impossible, for Murdoch to buy the *Financial Times* and Dow Jones if GE decided to step in, since Murdoch would no longer have to deal with just the Bancrofts but also execs from GE and Pearson.

But GE and Pearson, like all the other would-be suitors, could not make the numbers work. It took them only ten days after the announcement that they were exploring the deal to issue a press release officially bowing out of the running.

GE conceded that it and NBC Universal are "always evaluating opportunities to enhance our businesses and shareowner value, particularly when they involve superior global brands such as CNBC, the Financial Times Group and Dow Jones," and that GE and CNBC "recently held exploratory discussions with Pearson regarding a possible combination of these properties." But it added that "following these discussions, GE and Pearson have decided not to pursue this combination."

Pearson's release was worded very similarly to GE's. Translation: GE and Pearson would have loved to buy Dow Jones but could not justify to their shareholders why they should spend more than $5 billion for the company.

As one prospective buyer after another fell by the wayside, Wall Street quickly grew weary of the Bancrofts' fruitless attempts to keep Dow Jones away from Murdoch, all of which played exactly into his hands. All Murdoch had to do was sit back and wait for the Bancrofts to eventually realize that he was the only game in town.

Mark Boyar, manager of the Boyar Value mutual fund, said he sold his stake in Dow Jones when the stock was trading between $56 and $58 a share. He said he grew tired of the Bancrofts bickering among themselves about the deal. He did not trust the Bancrofts to ultimately do what was right for shareholders and agree to sell the company to News Corp.

"I wasn't going to wait around to see if they were going to do this deal. They are so unpredictable and such a dysfunctional family. I still scratch my head that there is so much concern about the deal. This is money from heaven for them, and being owned by News Corp. would allow the *Wall Street Journal* to keep growing. Rupert is not the devil they make him out to be," Boyar said.[12]

He added that Murdoch clearly knew what he was doing by offering as much as he did for Dow Jones because his bid easily scared away other suitors. "Nobody else is willing to pay $60 a share for Dow Jones. There is nobody willing to pay $50 a share," Boyar said.[13]

But even if there were buyers that wanted to pay $50 a share for Dow Jones, Dow Jones' board knew that it risked opening itself up to a shareholder uprising if it accepted a lower deal. Some thought investors would sue Dow Jones' board for spurning the deal. And Murdoch knew he had Dow Jones backed into a corner as well.

"If you get into a counterbidding situation, the directors of Dow Jones would have a real problem accepting a lower bid. They would be sued by shareholders. The company is in play and our best guess is that Rupert will prevail. He's the only logical buyer," said Larry Haverty, a portfolio manager and analyst with GAMCO Investors, an investment management firm that owned shares of both Dow Jones and News Corp.[14]

With that in mind, Dow Jones announced—one day before GE and Pearson officially pulled the plug on their possible joint bid for Dow Jones—that the Bancrofts were giving up the responsibility of direct negotiations with Murdoch and News Corp.

In a statement, Dow Jones said that "representatives of the Bancroft family have concluded that the best way to continue to evaluate the News Corporation proposal to acquire the Company would be for the Board of Directors to take the lead in addressing all aspects of the proposal and all other strategic alternatives, including remaining independent."

The company talked tough. The Bancrofts "reiterated that any transaction must include appropriate provisions with respect to journalistic and editorial independence and integrity" and that "any acquisition will require the approval of the Board of Directors and shareholders owning a majority of the Company's voting power." But the decision to have the board, and not the Bancrofts, work on the deal with News Corp. was widely viewed by media experts and investors as an admission that Murdoch's victory was inevitable and imminent.

Still, nothing came smoothly in the battle for Dow Jones. And Murdoch had a couple more hurdles to leap before he could finally call the *Wall Street Journal* his own.

First, there was a growing sense that even though the Dow Jones' board would likely agree to a deal, Murdoch still could fail to get the votes of enough of the Bancroft family members needed to win approval from a majority of the company's controlling shareholders.

Some of the Bancrofts chafed at the idea of selling Dow Jones to Murdoch because of his reputation of heavy-handedness—

his reputation for making sure his various news properties issued stories that mirrored his conservative views.

Many of the Bancrofts were also very loyal to and supportive of their employees, particularly those in the IAPE union who were heavily against the notion of selling to News Corp.

In fact, some IAPE members even went as far as to stage a sick-out on June 28, 2007. Several reporters at the *Wall Street Journal* decided not to go to work that day, an action that the union described as a way to "demonstrate our conviction that the *Journal's* editorial integrity depends on an owner committed to journalistic independence."[15]

The union added that its members were worried that Dow Jones' "long tradition of independence, which has been the hallmark of our news coverage for decades, is threatened."[16]

This forced Murdoch to become slightly more conciliatory than he was probably used to being. But that didn't happen until after he first threatened to walk away from the deal.

According to an interview with *Time* magazine in late June 2007, Murdoch sounded downright apoplectic about the thought that he would have to share key decision-making duties with the Bancrofts.

"They're taking five billion dollars out of me and want to keep control in an industry in crisis! They can't sell their company and still control it—that's not how it works. I'm sorry!" the *Time* article quoted Murdoch as screaming to an unnamed person on the phone.[17]

David Joyce, an analyst who follows News Corp. for Wall Street investment bank Miller Tabak + Company, said at the time that it was silly for the Bancrofts to make as many demands as they did. Joyce did not believe Murdoch would kowtow to all of the Bancrofts' demands and that he shouldn't have to.

"The Bancroft family wants some controlling say in the independence of the editorial boards at Dow Jones. But obviously, if News Corp. is paying $5 billion they want control. That's logical," Joyce said.[18]

Ultimately, after several rounds of meetings with Dow Jones' board, Murdoch agreed to a deal in late June that guaranteed some level of editorial independence in the newsroom of the *Journal* and other Dow Jones publications. And in mid-July, News Corp. and Dow Jones reached a tentative agreement on the acquisition of the company.

Yet, even that was not enough to finally seal the deal for Murdoch. Weeks passed as various far-flung members of the Bancroft family continued to hem and haw about whether they should agree to sell to News Corp.

One of the Bancrofts most dead-set against the deal, Dow Jones director Christopher Bancroft, was said to be talking with hedge funds, private equity shops and other investors in a desperate attempt to convince them to buy shares of Dow Jones so they could vote against the deal.

Another director representing the Bancroft family, Leslie Hill, was said to be pressuring the company to meet with Burkle about resuscitating the possibility of him making an offer for Dow Jones.

And with a self-imposed deadline of five p.m. EST on July 30 to vote on whether to approve a deal rapidly approaching, reports surfaced that yet another branch of the Bancroft family, a trust based in Denver that represented about 9 percent of Dow Jones' voting shares, was holding out for News Corp. to raise its bid for the Class B shares owned mainly by Bancroft family members. These members were asking News Corp. to pay a 10 to 20 percent premium on top of the $60 a share already offered.

In other words, these Bancroft members were demanding between $66 and $72 per share for their Dow Jones shares. Murdoch, not surprisingly, balked at the request. One fund manager who sold his stake in Dow Jones before the merger was approved said he was stunned by the audacity of the Denver Bancrofts' demand. He said it must have been easy for Murdoch to call the Bancrofts' bluff.

"Murdoch is coming out to put some last-minute pressure on the Bancrofts. It's surprising that the family has taken so long to make a decision. How long does it take to make a vote with this kind of money on the table?" said Michael Chren, manager of the Allegiant Large Cap Value Fund. Chren said he sold his stake in Dow Jones in July at an average price of $58 per share.[19]

Chren argued that unless the Bancrofts were able to come up with a last-minute buyer for Dow Jones, they had no choice but to accept the deal. He added there was no way Murdoch would need to raise his offer.

"Why bid against yourself?" Chren said. "The stock would go back to the low $40s or high $30s in a meltdown if the Bancrofts reject the deal."[20]

Several Bancroft members ultimately came to this realization, and at long last Murdoch was able finally to declare triumphantly that he had succeeded in his quest to take over the *Journal*.

On July 31, 2007, News Corp. and Dow Jones issued a press release stating that the two companies had signed a definitive agreement to merge. Murdoch wound up not needing to raise his $60-per-share offer for the company, but the final value of the deal worked out to be $5.6 billion, as opposed to $5 billion, after factoring in the assumption of Dow Jones' debt.

The companies said that "certain members of the Bancroft family and the trustees of trusts for their benefit who collectively own approximately 37 percent of Dow Jones' voting stock have agreed to vote to approve the transaction."[21] So Murdoch did not win over all the Bancrofts, but he got the necessary support to ensure that he would not have a problem receiving a majority of the voting shares when the deal was brought to all Dow Jones stakeholders. Few Dow Jones shareholders outside of the Bancroft family opposed the News Corp. bid.

But Murdoch did concede a little on the editorial-control front. As part of the merger agreement, News Corp. and Dow Jones also "agreed on the terms of an editorial agreement that provides for the establishment of a five-member, special committee with the objective of assuring the continued journalistic and editorial integrity and independence of Dow Jones' publications and services."[22]

Murdoch was gracious in victory and attempted to try and make amends for some of the bad blood that was generated during the three-month-long fight for Dow Jones.

"I am deeply gratified at the level of support we have received from the Bancroft family and its trustees. Given the Bancrofts' long and distinguished history as custodians of Dow Jones, we appreciate how difficult this decision was for some family members. I want to offer the Bancrofts my thanks, and an assurance that our company and my family will be equally strong custodians," Murdoch said in the press release.[23]

To that end, News Corp. also agreed to appoint a member of the Bancroft family to News Corp.'s board upon the deal's closing, which was set for early December 2007. Still, the Bancrofts were not completely mollified. In a separate statement, a spokesman for the Bancroft family said that "the process of thoroughly reviewing a broad range of possible alternatives for Dow Jones has been long, complex and arduous."

The family added that "it is our most fervent hope that in the years to come, the *Wall Street Journal* will continue to enjoy, and deserve, the universal admiration and respect in which it is held all over the world, and that the *Journal* and Dow Jones's other print and online publications will continue to achieve great things as part of a larger, well-capitalized, global organization committed to upholding the long tradition of journalistic excellence, independence and editorial integrity of which we are all so proud."

Leslie Hill, a key director representing the interest of the Bancrofts, resigned as a Dow Jones director the day the merger was agreed to because she did not back the deal. In a letter to the board, she said the deal's good financial terms didn't offset "the loss of an independent global news organization with unmatched credibility and integrity."

Nonetheless, Murdoch still had the battle won. And even though he would have to wait until December before Dow Jones would officially become part of the News Corp. media empire, he was already busy trying to make the *Wall Street Journal* more profitable and improve its appeal to a broader audience.

During the company's fiscal fourth-quarter conference call on August 8, 2007, a little more than a week after the ink on the Dow Jones merger agreement dried, Murdoch said he saw an opportunity to cut $50 million in expenses at Dow Jones. Looking to dispel the notion that massive layoffs were coming, Murdoch said later during the same call that the cuts in expenses would not come from firing people.

But just a month later, speaking at a Goldman Sachs media conference, Murdoch said that News Corp. had "already identified low-hanging fruit" at Dow Jones and now saw up to $100 million in savings.[24]

In August, Murdoch also said that he planned to invest heavily in Asia and Europe and that in order to compete more effectively with the *New York Times* and other leading papers, Dow Jones publications, particularly the *Journal*, would need to add more coverage of "national, international and nonbusiness news."[25]

That comment appeared to confirm the worst fears of many Murdoch critics. Ever since News Corp. announced its intention to buy Dow Jones in May 2007, many media observers argued that Murdoch was not really interested in being the business journalism leader but that he wanted the *Journal* as yet another means to promote his business and political interests in the United States and abroad.

In particular, with China as an increasingly attractive market for Murdoch's growing global satellite television and digital media interests, the concern was how the paper would cover China. After all, a team of reporters for the *Journal* in China won the 2007 Pulitzer Prize for international reporting. The Pulitzer committee described their coverage as "sharply edged reports on the adverse impact of China's booming capitalism on conditions ranging from inequality to pollution." Would the *Journal* continue to take a hard look at China or would Murdoch not allow it?

"This deal holds great promise and great peril for the *Wall Street Journal*. The peril for the company is Murdoch's reputation. If he started to meddle in an unseemly way, that would hurt," said Rich Hanley, assistant professor of journalism and director of graduate programs at Quinnipiac University's

School of Communications, on the day of the merger agreement.[26]

Along those lines, Free Press, a national nonpartisan group whose aim is to reform the media, had urged the Bancrofts to reject Murdoch's offer. Free Press argued that allowing Murdoch to control the *Journal* would give him even more power and influence than he already enjoyed.

"Rupert Murdoch's takeover of the *Wall Street Journal* may not be illegal, but it's certainly wrong. The cost of giving one company—and one man—this much media power is simply too high," said Free Press president Robert W. McChesney in a statement written two weeks before News Corp. and Dow Jones finally agreed to a merger.[27]

"Less than a dozen outlets—the major TV networks, a few cable news channels and a couple of newspapers—set the national news agenda. They decide what most citizens will—or will not—learn. If this deal goes through, Murdoch would control three of them: the Fox Network, Fox News Channel and the *Journal*. And that is just the tip of the iceberg for his media empire. When is it enough?" McChesney continued.[28]

Reporters at Dow Jones also had reason to worry. Shortly after News Corp. announced its bid for Dow Jones in May, Murdoch was quoted in a story in the *New York Times* as saying that he thought many articles in the *Journal* were too long and that he rarely got around to finishing some articles.

That concerned IAPE union president Steve Yount. He

wrote in a letter to fellow union members that he "was particularly troubled" by Murdoch's comments.

"I'm afraid Mr. Murdoch doesn't understand why *The Wall Street Journal* is *The Wall Street Journal*. Not everything is five paragraphs and [a] picture. Dow Jones did not become the most trusted source of business news and information in the world by serving up News Nuggets," Yount wrote.

But many other media experts were bemused by the criticism of Murdoch and felt that Murdoch was savvy enough to realize that if he changed the tenor of the *Journal*'s editorial scope and coverage too drastically, he would risk alienating and losing readers—and advertisers.

"The notion that Murdoch will trash the *Journal* and put nude models on the front page is just silly. He is a savvy and successful media operator," said James Owers, a professor of finance at the Robinson College of Business at Georgia State University, who follows media mergers closely.[29]

Hanley conceded that there was legitimate reason to worry about the changes Murdoch might make at Dow Jones. But he thought Murdoch would be careful not to go too far since the *Journal*'s core group of readers—professional businesspeople and high-level executives—would be smart enough to realize what was going on.

"Readers are too sophisticated for cheerleading and that would be self-defeating. So there is an inherent self-correcting mechanism," he said.[30]

Murdoch himself was not deaf to the complaints and critiques. During the earnings conference call in August 2007, he bemoaned the way that he was vilified in many news accounts of the Dow Jones takeover saga. At one point, he said that he felt he endured criticism that was more befitting of a "genocidal tyrant."[31]

Murdoch was quick to try and reassure the financial community, including, of course, the many employees at the *Journal* and other Dow Jones publications, that much of the speculation about what he would do to Dow Jones was simply not true.

He touted Dow Jones' "unassailable credibility" and said that was one reason why he had paid such a big premium for Dow Jones in the first place. When asked by a reporter if he planned to license the Dow Jones name for use in other products, Murdoch quipped that "you're not going to see Dow Jones T-shirts and hats."[32]

Murdoch seemed to realize that even though he wanted to see more coverage of politics and international events, business news was Dow Jones' greatest strength. To that end, Murdoch said he would look for synergies between Dow Jones and other News Corp. businesses, most notably the company's upcoming Fox Business Network, which was set to launch in October 2007.

Murdoch promised to make Dow Jones an even bigger player in online journalism once the deal officially closed.

Along those lines, Murdoch added that News Corp. was talking with Dow Jones about possibly making the *Journal*'s

Web site, which at the time kept a lot of its content behind a "walled garden" only available to paying subscribers, free to all readers.

The issue of whether the *Wall Street Journal*'s content should be free online was a subject of intense debate in media circles. On the one hand, many media experts argued that the *Journal* needed to go free in order to generate more traffic to the site, and thus more advertising revenue. Others countered that readers should pay to access the site, given the quality of the *Journal*'s stories, and that even if Dow Jones was sacrificing some page views in the process, it was worth it because of the stability that would come from recurring subscription fees.

In September, at the Goldman Sachs media conference, Murdoch said that he was leaning toward making everything on the *Journal*'s site free, since that appeared to be "the way the industry was going . . . free news supported by advertising." Murdoch added that a key to the Dow Jones deal was making sure that readers were not forced to have online subscriptions tied to subscriptions for the print publication.

"Dow Jones is a great challenge but it presents enormous opportunities. We don't mind what platform the stories appear on. We're platform neutral—newsprint, your BlackBerry, your PC, whatever," he said.[33]

Still, it would take a few months for Murdoch to decide how best to tackle this dilemma. Ultimately, he decided to take a hybrid approach, following the lead of other prominent newspapers such as the *New York Times* and the *Financial Times*, which opened up many portions of their Web sites to all readers but did not give away all content for free.

During an earnings conference call in February 2008, Murdoch said that News Corp. had decided to make the *Journal's* opinion pieces and blogs free to nonsubscribers but that "the bulk of the core business coverage will remain behind the subscription wall." This, Murdoch stressed, would enable the newspaper to "broaden its reach while increasing subscription revenue."[34]

But Murdoch quickly added that he was not done making changes at Dow Jones. He said that more free content would be added to the online version of the *Journal*. "More changes are in the works for Dow Jones. Changes attract more readers and advertisers, allowing us to outperform the general newspaper industry," Murdoch said. "We will strengthen our online assets. That is where we are spending most of our concentrated time."[35]

Murdoch reiterated this stance at a Bear Stearns media conference in March. He stressed that "Dow Jones has a huge opportunity on the Internet" and added that the company's financial news is among "the most valuable information in the world" and that it's up to News Corp. to "expand faster and faster" on the Web. Murdoch also conceded that he did not think Dow Jones would be "as big a profit center going forward" as other News Corp. businesses. He said it may be "fairly big" but would not be nearly as profitable as Fox News, for example.[36]

Comments like that would appear to validate the notion that Murdoch really wasn't buying Dow Jones to enhance News Corp.'s shareholder value as much as he was trying to enhance his influence in the world through the *Wall Street Journal*'s coverage. And since Dow Jones was taken over by News Corp., there have been some notable changes at the paper.

But the majority of the changes made at Dow Jones in the first few months under Murdoch were cosmetic in nature.

The paper did showcase its political coverage more prominently than it had in the past and there was also more use of photos in addition to the paper's trademark black-and-white drawings.

Murdoch also brought in some of his most trusted executives from his global newspaper division to oversee the management of Dow Jones. Richard Zannino, who had been Dow Jones' chief executive officer and was widely credited for starting more productive merger talks with Murdoch when the Bancrofts had reached a stalemate, announced he was leaving Dow Jones on December 7, 2007, six days before News Corp. officially completed the acquisition.

Murdoch replaced Zannino with Les Hinton, a lifetime News Corp. employee who began his career at the company as a reporter with the *Adelaide News* and worked his way through News Corp.'s newspaper ranks to eventually become the chairman of News International, overseeing Murdoch's British publications, including the *Times*, the *Sunday Times*, the *Sun*, *News of the World*, the *Times Literary Supplement* and *thelondonpaper*, a free newspaper.

Murdoch described Hinton, in an announcement about his new role, as "one of the most respected executives in the media industry" who "had a great record of introducing innovations that have been replicated by other newspaper companies around the world."[37]

In addition, Murdoch appointed Robert Thomson, who had been the editor of Murdoch's *Times* since March 2002 and prior to that was a reporter and editor at the *Financial Times* for nearly two decades, as Dow Jones' publisher. The managing editor and editorial page editor of the *Wall Street Journal*, the managing editor of Dow Jones Newswires, as well as the editors of *Barron's* and MarketWatch.com all report to Thomson.

Murdoch touted Thomson's "brilliant editorial instincts" and said that they, "combined with his keen sense of the marketplace, will be tremendously valuable at this critical stage in the expansion of the *Wall Street Journal* and the other Dow Jones properties."[38] Thomson was subsequently named editor in chief of the *Journal* in May 2008.

Murdoch also lived up to his promise about keeping the Bancrofts involved with the company, naming Natalie Bancroft as a director of News Corp. But even that move was met with skepticism and head-scratching in media circles, as Natalie Bancroft, a twenty-seven-year-old professionally trained opera singer living in Italy, had little experience in the media business.

With changes to the board set, the merger was finally completed on December 13. And with Dow Jones now officially part of the News Corp. family, Murdoch had at long last emerged victorious. But in many respects, the battle surrounding Dow Jones was just beginning. Now Murdoch had to convince many cynical shareholders and Wall Street analysts that the deal was the right one.

At a media mergers conference in New York City in late June 2007, a spirited discussion about the merits of the deal took place.

Norman Pearlstine, who at the time was a senior adviser with the Carlyle Group, a prominent buyout firm, said the deal did not make sense for News Corp., particularly at such a high price. It's a potentially biased opinion, considering that Pearlstine used to be an editor at the *Journal* and later went on to lead Time Inc.

Pearlstine said he thought the *Wall Street Journal* wouldn't help Murdoch's plan to start Fox Business. He argued that the *Journal*'s brand name wouldn't necessarily translate to television. In addition, there was the issue of Dow Jones still having a relationship with CNBC until 2011.

Pearlstine added that if Dow Jones was really such an important asset that had to be kept away from Murdoch, then GE, Pearson or even McGraw-Hill, which owns *BusinessWeek* and

Standard & Poor's, should have been willing to match, or even top, Murdoch's bid.

"There are some obvious people out there that could have done a deal. You would think Dow Jones would be more valuable to GE in order to protect CNBC," Pearlstine said, also noting that private equity firms had been notably absent in the recent round of newspaper consolidation, suggesting that the newspaper publishing business was not that attractive.[39]

Laura Martin, founder and CEO of Media Metrics, a sell-side research firm that covers media companies, agreed with Pearlstine. At the time, she had a "sell" rating on News Corp. and said that a deal for Dow Jones would "destroy value" for News Corp. shareholders. Her argument was that by adding Dow Jones, News Corp. would increase its exposure to the slow-growth newspaper business.

But Murdoch had his defenders also. At that same conference, John Chachas, managing director of media and telecommunications at investment bank Lazard, said a combination of News Corp. and Dow Jones was a "brilliant deal." His primary rationale was that the deal would help News Corp. as it sought to launch Fox Business later in the year.[40]

And Richard Bilotti, formerly the longtime media and entertainment analyst for Morgan Stanley, said that even though he thought the deal was expensive, it would pay off for Murdoch in the long run. He argued that critics of the deal were focusing too much on the price tag attached to the deal as well as the weakening newspaper business and the short-term benefits.

Bilotti believed Murdoch offered as much as he did because he was thinking about what Dow Jones could earn under his management in three to five years, not in the next quarter.[41]

An investor in News Corp. said in July 2007 that he also thought criticism of the deal was unfounded. "I'm not really worried. This is a one-off deal since Dow Jones is a trophy franchise," said Scott Black, president of Delphi Management, which owned about 475,000 shares of News Corp. in July 2007. "This is not indicative that News Corp.'s going to go out and buy Gannett, for example, or make more investments in traditional newspapers."[42]

Black added that he thought the Dow Jones acquisition, while pricey, made sense for News Corp. because owning Dow Jones could help lead to a stronger debut for the Fox Business Channel once it launched. He said there were opportunities for cost cutting as well as the ability to cross-promote Dow Jones publications not just on Fox Business but also on Fox News and its global satellite networks. "I realize synergy is a word that's bandied about a lot. But there are a lot of opportunities to extract value from Dow Jones," Black said.[43]

Media investment banker Reed Phillips of DeSilva & Phillips agreed with that assessment. "This is an aberration. I wouldn't even lump the *Wall Street Journal* and Dow Jones in with other newspapers in general. The characteristics of the *Journal* are quite a bit different from daily newspapers. It's a national business publication and that's why Murdoch wanted it. I don't think Dow Jones is being impacted by the same forces bringing valuations down at other newspaper publishers," he said.[44]

Still, concerns about the wisdom of the deal continued after News Corp. and Dow Jones finally agreed to a merger in August. Martin, in a report from late November, reiterated her "sell" rating on News Corp. She took a hard look at the areas where News Corp. had been investing its capital in the past few years and believed Murdoch was making some key mistakes.

She noted that the company's newspaper business and book publishing divisions had both experienced a huge increase in capital spending over the past few years even though these divisions had among the lowest returns on assets—ROAs—for News Corp.'s divisions. Capital expenditures in the newspaper division (not including the Dow Jones purchase) had nearly doubled since fiscal 2004.

Martin argued that the company's focus on its slow-growth newspaper business overshadowed the rapid growth in News Corp.'s Fox Interactive Media unit, which includes social network MySpace, gaming site IGN and image hosting and sharing site Photobucket.

"Segments with the lowest ROAs and slowest earnings growth have reported the highest increases in capital spending since fiscal 2004," she wrote. "With no reprieve from higher capital intensity in sight, we recommend investors avoid [News Corp.] shares at current price levels."

She was not alone in her skepticism. In a broad overview of the media sector's prospects for 2008, published in December

2007, Bear Stearns analyst Spencer Wang wrote that the Dow Jones deal was not "a particularly good use of capital for News Corp." and that he did not "believe that the deal will create value for News Corp. shareholders."

And the weak debut of the Fox Business Network may have also put some cracks in the argument that the decision to buy Dow Jones was sound because of the favorable impact it could have on the launch of Fox Business. According to television ratings research firm Nielsen Media Research, it could not officially disclose the initial ratings for Fox Business during its first two months on the air because they failed to meet Nielsen's average minimum threshold of 35,000 viewers a day.

One television expert, speaking on the day of the Fox Business launch, predicted that the ratings would be low at first but said it would be a mistake to bet against Murdoch and Ailes, particularly because of Ailes's time with CNBC.

"Obviously, we have to wait and see on the Nielsen numbers and it will be a little while before Nielsen gets them on the radar," said Jordan Breslow, director of broadcast research with Mediacom, a media buying firm owned by ad agency WPP Group. "But there is no reason to think Fox wouldn't thrive since they have people behind the network who know what they are doing. Competition is always healthy and there is only one other major player in cable business news."[45]

Murdoch was not deterred by the mounting criticism of the company's bet on Dow Jones and Fox Business. During the company's fiscal second-quarter 2008 earnings conference call in February 2008, Murdoch and Chernin indicated they were comfortable with how Fox Business was doing, saying that they were not surprised by the low ratings and that the network was losing less money than they had budgeted for at this time.

Plus, for a company of News Corp.'s size, spending $5.6 billion on Dow Jones and a couple hundred million to launch Fox Business won't break the bank. "Rupert's not betting the whole company on this acquisition," said James McGlynn, manager of the Summit Everest Fund, which owned about 44,000 shares of News Corp., shortly after Dow Jones finally agreed to the deal in August 2007.[46]

But McGlynn added that he did not expect the Dow Jones transaction to have a material impact, positive or negative, on earnings anytime soon for the company. And that all leads back to the question of whether the purchase of Dow Jones really was worth it in the first place. Will owning Dow Jones really enhance shareholder value for News Corp. investors, or was the whole bidding process merely a vanity project for Murdoch?

Only time will tell if the deal does yield dividends for News Corp. or if it was simply a $5.6 billion ego boost for Murdoch. Either way, the consequences of buying Dow Jones is something that is likely to be dealt with by someone other than Murdoch. Although Murdoch is showing no signs of slowing down, he is now seventy-eight. And he has already started to set the stage for a successor.

CHAPTER 8

All in the Family

"I just want to live forever," Murdoch said in February 2007. He's said that on numerous occasions before and he's likely to keep saying it. One gets the impression that Murdoch must think that if he continues to talk about immortality, he might actually find a way to achieve it.

Murdoch is also fond of pointing to the example of his mother, Dame Elisabeth Murdoch, who turned ninety-nine in February 2007 and is still quite active herself. In other words, Rupert could very well serve as News Corp.'s chairman and CEO for another decade or so.

"Keep busy morning, noon and night," Dame Elisabeth said to reporters at a birthday party in Melbourne, Australia, shortly before her birthday in February 2007. "I'm sure it is far better to be busier than you would imagine possible. We all do better when we are a bit switched on," she added.[1]

But unless Murdoch can succeed where sixteenth-century

Spanish explorer Ponce de León failed (he searched fruitlessly for the Fountain of Youth), then it is pointless for Murdoch to act as if he does not need to plan for succession.

At most publicly traded companies, finding a new chief executive officer and chairman is a matter for the firm's board of directors to decide. News Corp., of course, is no exception. But News Corp. is also Murdoch's legacy. His two sons, Lachlan and James, are both members of News Corp.'s board. And Murdoch has made it no secret that he expects a Murdoch to lead News Corp. after he steps down.

"It's a matter for the board but they better take into account what shareholders think. My family has about 40 percent ownership," Murdoch said in early 2007.

At one time, Lachlan, the older son, was presumed to be Murdoch's successor. But amid reports of a growing rift between Rupert and Lachlan regarding frustration about Rupert's management style, Lachlan stepped down as deputy chief operating officer in August 2005.

"I have today resigned my executive position at News Corporation. I will remain on the board and I am excited about my continued involvement with the Company in a different role. I look forward to returning home to Australia with my wife, Sarah, and son, Kalan, in the very near future. I would like especially to thank my father for all he has taught me in business and in life. It is now time for me to apply those lessons to the next phase of my career," Lachlan said in a statement.[2]

Rupert said later in the statement that he was "particularly saddened by my son's decision and [I] thank him for his terrific contribution to the Company, and also his agreement to stay on the board and advise us in a number of areas. I have respected the professionalism and integrity that he has exhibited throughout his career at News Corporation. His achievements include driving all of his reporting divisions to record profits and the *New York Post* to its highest-ever circulation. I am grateful that I will continue to have the benefit of Lachlan's counsel and wisdom in his continued role on the Company's board."[3]

Lachlan eventually founded his own investment firm in Australia called Illyria. And in January 2008, Lachlan made his first attempt toward building his own media empire. Not surprisingly, he followed his father's lead and sought to acquire a company with interests in the publishing, pay television, cable network and Internet businesses.

Illyria announced that it was teaming with Consolidated Press Holdings (CPH), a media firm run by James Packer, the son of the late Australian billionaire Kerry Packer, to bid for Consolidated Media Holdings (CMH). CMH, a publicly traded company, has stakes in Australian cable TV company Foxtel, magazine publisher and TV network owner PBL Media and Australian jobs site Seek.com. It also has a stake in Premier Media Group, which is a co-owner of Fox Sports in Australia.

CPH already owned a 38 percent stake in Consolidated Media Holdings. The Illyria-CPH offer valued CMH's stock at a 30 percent premium above where the shares were trading the day before the offer, demonstrating that Lachlan had probably learned from his father that overpaying for an asset is a way to ensure that you can succeed in your takeover attempt. In another cue from Rupert, Lachlan indicated that he was not going to be negotiating with CMH, terming the Illyria offer as "final."

"We are well-positioned to work with the co-owners of Consolidated Media Holdings' existing portfolio businesses to invest in and develop these assets," Lachlan said in a statement about the offer. And in a bit of hubris, another trait probably inherited from his father, Lachlan touted Illyria's "unique combination of experience in pay TV, broadcast and print media" as being able to give CMH the ability for "new growth opportunities in the long-term." Illyria was only established in 2005 and the CMH bid was the company's first major foray into the media business, having previously only established a joint venture with Indian public relations firm Percept Group to set up a talent agency for celebrities and athletes in 2007.

The CMH deal hit a snag in March 2008 when SPO Partners, an American private investment firm, changed its mind about providing some financial backing to Illyria and Packer. A month later Lachlan Murdoch and Packer pulled out of the deal for CMH, since they were unable to find a new partner. But even with the bid failing, Lachlan is still presumably out of the succession picture now that he's shown he wants to build his own mini News Corp.

Murdoch also has two older daughters: Prudence, whom Murdoch had during his first marriage, to Patricia Booker; and Elisabeth, who along with Lachlan and James is the child of

Murdoch and his second wife, Anna Torv. Prudence was never involved heavily in News Corp. businesses. But Elisabeth was, like her brothers, an active player at News Corp. She was a managing director at BSkyB from 1996 to 2000 and was responsible for overseeing nonsports-related programming and consumer marketing. However, Elisabeth, like Lachlan, has also shown something of an independent streak.

She left BSkyB in 2000 and in 2001 formed Shine Limited, an independent television production company that BSkyB has a minority stake in. "I have enjoyed my four years at Sky enormously. It is a company that I have been proud to work for and contribute to. At Sky, I have had the privilege of working with some of the best television executives around and it is with some lament that I leave such a winning team. However, now is a great time to pursue something that I have been thinking about for some time," Elisabeth said in a statement about her departure from Sky.[4]

So unless Rupert decides to stay on as chairman and CEO of News Corp. for the next twenty or so years, long enough for his youngest daughters Chloe and Grace to grow up and have their names thrown into the succession chatter, then it is looking increasingly likely that youngest son James will eventually be the new leader of News Corp.

This notion was further cemented in 2007 when James announced he was stepping down as the head of BSkyB to take over as the chairman and CEO of News Corp.'s European and Asian operations. Not surprisingly, there was the same uproar about this decision as there was four years earlier when James was tapped to be the CEO of BSkyB in 2003. At that time, there were predictable cries of nepotism, and Rupert Murdoch, as is usually the case, had to quickly fire back and address the criticism.

"The Board and I are pleased that the Nomination Committee has completed its task and it is unanimous in its conviction that James is the right man for this job. He follows a series of successful Chief Executives—Sam Chisholm, Mark Booth and Tony Ball. I feel confident that James will carry on their work and continue the company's success," Rupert Murdoch said in a statement announcing James's appointment.[5]

James Murdoch's immediate predecessor, Tony Ball, described James as "an outstanding executive whom I know has the ability and drive to take the company forward." And James Murdoch, calling Sky "one of a very small group of Britain's great new industrial companies," pledged to keep the company on top of the satellite television business in the United Kingdom and make it even stronger in the years to come.[6]

"It is a world leader in multichannel television and an innovative business which has, since its inception, been at the forefront in technological and creative advance. It is a privilege to have the opportunity to play a part in the company's future. I particularly look forward to working with the people at Sky who have played such a key role in its success, and to working for all the shareholders to deliver even greater value," James Murdoch said.[7]

For what it's worth, analysts have said that James Murdoch

did an admirable job during his time at the top at BSkyB. Because he'd proved himself to be an able executive at BSkyB, News Corp. investors should have less reason for concern about his rise to the top of that company's executive ranks. While at BSkyB, James Murdoch made the bold move in 2006 to buy a 17.9 percent stake in competitor ITV, a move that was viewed as a smart strategic way to block ITV from merging with Richard Branson's Virgin Media cable company. Such a merger would have made Virgin a much more formidable threat to BSkyB. But BSkyB's investment in ITV also raised some antitrust concerns and the British government ordered BSkyB to reduce its stake in ITV to less than 7.5 percent in January 2008.

Still, James Murdoch's tenure was not an unmitigated success. Shares of BSkyB rose only about 10 percent during his four years as the CEO of BSkyB. By way of comparison, News Corp.'s stock rose about 15 percent during the same time frame. Both stocks, however, underperformed the broader market by a wide margin, as the benchmark S&P 500 index, of which News Corp. is a member, gained about 40 percent between November 2003 and December 2007.

But part of the reason for BSkyB's underperformance can be attributed to the fact that James Murdoch decided to invest heavily in building out BSkyB's broadband Internet and telephone offerings as British telecoms are beginning to become more aggressive competitors in video; this is similar to what's happened with the U.S. telecom and video landscape. This, in the long run, may turn out to be a smart strategic move. But in the short-term, the rollout of new services hurt profits and hence the stock. If nothing else, the decision to not stand still proved that James, like Rupert, is not afraid to take risks even if it means incurring the ire of investors in the process.

To be sure, BSkyB's stock price lagged behind News Corp.'s and the broader market during James Murdoch's overall tenure. But the stock took its biggest hit during the first two years he was in charge. In fact, BSkyB's stock outperformed the broader market throughout 2006 and 2007 and even topped the performance of News Corp. during those two years.

Still, there are questions as to whether James, who turned thirty-five in December 2007, is ready to assume the top spot at News Corp. if the opportunity presented itself in the next few years. Rupert himself conceded in February 2007 during his presentation at the McGraw-Hill conference that "it was too early to say if James could be a great chief executive officer."[8]

And running all of News Corp. is certainly a much more significant chore than simply running BSkyB. Although James Murdoch has been involved in many aspects of News Corp.'s global interests, he is still largely an unknown quantity to U.S. media observers and investors. And despite News Corp.'s global scope, the company does generate more than half of its total sales from the United States and is also a U.S.-based company.

If James Murdoch is going to one day run the entire company, he will need, at some point, to become more involved with the Fox broadcast network and movie studio as well as the company's thriving U.S. cable networks business.

What's more, investors should have legitimate concerns about whether James truly is the best person to succeed Rupert or if he will simply one day be rewarded the job because it is considered his birthright. Recent history suggests that there is a largely mixed track record of success with family-run media companies in the United States.

The *Washington Post* is perhaps the best example of a seamless transition within a family-run media company. Eugene Meyer, who bought the *Washington Post* in 1933, passed on the leadership of that company to his daughter Katharine Graham, who in her two decades running the company was hailed as one of the most important people in the news business. It was during her tenure that the *Washington Post* wrote its series of stories about the Watergate scandal in President Nixon's administration. The *Washington Post* is now led by Graham's son Donald, who took over as chairman and CEO in 1991. The *Washington Post*, thanks in part to investments outside of the media business, most notably the purchase of the educational testing company Kaplan, has consistently been one of the best-performing media stocks year in and year out.

Cable giant Comcast is another prime example of what happens when a son inherits the top spot from a parent to the investors' benefit. Current Comcast CEO Brian Roberts, who took over for his father, founder and chairman Ralph Roberts, is widely acknowledged as one of the savviest and most astute executives in the cable business. Under Brian Roberts's leadership, Comcast has made several acquisitions that enabled the company to go from being a primarily regional cable company to the largest cable firm in the United States.

But not all family-run media companies have happy endings for shareholders. While Graham and Roberts largely enjoy acclaim from investors and respect from their peers, the same cannot be said for Cablevision chief executive officer James Dolan, son of Cablevision founder and chairman Charles Dolan. James Dolan, who plays an active role in managing Cablevision's two professional sports franchises, the National Basketball Association's New York Knicks and National Hockey League's New York Rangers, is routinely lampooned by both the sports press and financial reporters for the teams' poor performances and his questionable decisions regarding both player and management personnel decisions. What's more, James Dolan and Charles Dolan were even involved in a public spat over Cablevision's decision to shut down a satellite television service it had launched. James was in favor of shuttering the service and Charles was not; the company's satellite and spectrum allocation was eventually sold to satellite television rival EchoStar.

Another family-run cable company, Adelphia, was driven into bankruptcy by founder John Rigas and his son, chief financial officer Timothy Rigas. In addition, both Rigases were convicted of securities fraud in 2004 and went to prison in August 2007. Adelphia was eventually sold piecemeal to Comcast and Time Warner.

It's of course too soon to say if James Murdoch will turn out to be more like Brian Roberts or James Dolan.

But James Murdoch has already made his mark on News Corp. He played an active role in making News Corp. a "greener" company. In January 2008, James Murdoch announced that News International, the main British subsidiary of News Corp. and owner of all the company's U.K.-based newspapers, had cut its carbon emissions by 21 percent over the prior year and was in the process of going "carbon neutral," having net zero carbon emissions.

"This is a major milestone for News International, but it is only a beginning. The key to any company's environmental program is to improve energy efficiency and we have a lot more to do in this area. But this is a good start and I am glad to say our suppliers are working hard to implement best energy practices as well. As a major media company we reach a wide audience both in the U.K. and worldwide. It is important that we get the message across to our readers, advertisers, business partners and staff that we are making good progress on an issue we, and they, care a great deal about," James Murdoch said in a statement.[9]

The program is actually part of News Corp.'s broader Global Energy Initiative, which the company describes as an "effort to play its part in solving the climate problem by transforming its operations' use of energy, by engaging its millions of readers, viewers and Web users on environmental issues." The company is planning to have all units go entirely carbon neutral by 2010 and James Murdoch has been widely credited with helping his father find new religion in going "green."

During a speech in Tokyo in November 2006, Rupert Murdoch said that "until recently, I was somewhat wary of the warming debate," but that he now felt a "responsibility to take the lead on this issue." He praised James, who at the time was still the head of BSkyB, for "making his company carbon neutral" and proving that "being environmentally sound is not sentimentality. It is a sound business strategy and an example that the whole of News Corporation is striving to emulate."[10]

When Rupert Murdoch announced the Global Energy Initiative in May 2007, there were points where he almost sounded like Al Gore, which is of course ironic given how the former vice president and presidential candidate was routinely pilloried by the *New York Post* and Fox News.

"If we are to connect with our audiences on this issue, we must first get our own house in order. We have just begun this effort, and we have a long way to go. Our global reach gives us an unprecedented opportunity to inspire action from all corners of the world. The climate problem will not be solved without mass participation by the general public everywhere," Rupert Murdoch said.[11]

Nonetheless, despite James Murdoch's early efforts to make News Corp. a more environmentally friendly company and his apparent willingness to reach out to his father's rivals, some analysts believe he has a long way to go before proving that he can manage the entire company. In addition, now that he is once again overseeing business operations in China, his remarks about Falun Gong being a "dangerous" cult could come back to haunt him as allegations that he, like his father, may exert influence through News Corp.'s media holdings in order to win favor with the Chinese government will clearly not die down.

During testimony to the House of Lords in January 2008, Andrew Neil, formerly a longtime editor of News Corp.'s *Sunday Times*, conceded that he did not believe James Murdoch has "the same strong views on politics" as his father but said that it was fair to assume that James Murdoch might act in a similar manner—using his editorial influence to advance the company's business interests—as Rupert.

"I assume that part of the reason he got the job was because of his DNA, so I am sure that part of it [the need to exert control] is in the DNA," Neil quipped.[12]

That all leads to what is perhaps the biggest question facing News Corp. shareholders these days. At the risk of sounding morbid, if Rupert Murdoch were to get struck dead by lightning or face some health problem that rendered him incapable of continuing to act as chairman and CEO of News Corp., who would take over? Is James Murdoch ready for that role or would a caretaker CEO need to be brought in until James Murdoch is in fact ready to assume his father's spot as the head of News Corp.?

Enter Peter Chernin. Chernin has been a trusted and loyal News Corp. executive since he joined the company in 1989 as the president of entertainment for Fox Broadcasting and was promoted to chief executive officer of Fox Filmed Entertainment in 1992. Since 1996, he has been Rupert's second in command, serving as president and chief operating officer of News Corp.

It's tough to imagine how News Corp. could have grown to the position that it enjoys today, particularly in the United States, without Chernin's involvement. During his time as the head of the Fox network, the network launched several shows that helped put the fledgling network on the map, including *The Simpsons* and *Beverly Hills 90210*. And while overseeing the film studio, Fox released several huge box office hits, including *Speed*, *Mrs. Doubtfire*, *True Lies*, *Independence Day* and the biggest-grossing movie of all-time, *Titanic*, which Fox coproduced with Viacom-owned Paramount.

Chernin has often been mentioned as a prime candidate for one day becoming the CEO of a major media company—but not News Corp., since it is so widely assumed that a younger Murdoch will one day take over for Rupert.

But even prior to Lachlan Murdoch's departure from News Corp. in 2005, it appeared that Rupert Murdoch realized that in Chernin he had a capable executive whom he had better retain rather than let jump ship to a competitor.

As a result, Chernin signed a new five-year contract with News Corp. in July 2004, a contract to keep him as president and chief operating officer of the company through June 2009. Murdoch spoke glowingly of Chernin when announcing the new contract.

"Peter has been a close and trusted colleague for more than a decade and I am delighted that News Corporation will continue to have the benefit of his dynamic qualities for many years to come. He has done a superb job growing and operating our core entertainment businesses in an increasingly challenging global marketplace. Peter is respected throughout our company and the industry for his intelligence, drive and leadership," Murdoch said.[13]

And for his part, Chernin said that he felt privileged to work with "the most talented, creative and aggressive management team in the business" and added that "I'm also enormously fortunate to have worked side by side with Rupert as News Corporation has become a global media company that today is without a peer, and I look forward to building on our successes over the next several years."[14]

Still, even though Chernin appeared to now be locked up for the next few years, that didn't stop people from chattering about the possibility of him leaving if a CEO job opportunity presented itself. That's because according to the details of his new contract, filed with the Securities and Exchange Commission in November 2004, Chernin was allowed to leave News Corp. without giving notice if he wanted to become the CEO of another publicly traded company. If he wanted to leave to head a private company or a unit of another publicly traded firm, he would have to give six months' notice.

At the time, this was interpreted as a way for Chernin to opt out of his contract if the CEO position at Walt Disney opened up, which it did. However, Disney decided to stay in-house and named its own president and chief operating officer Robert Iger to succeed Michael Eisner as CEO in March 2005.

With the Disney job no longer an option, it's harder to imagine where Chernin might go if he were to leave News Corp. Sumner Redstone has shown no inkling as of late that he is looking to replace either Leslie Moonves or Philippe Dauman at CBS and Viacom, respectively. Time Warner had a smooth transition of its own with longtime president and chief operating officer Jeffrey Bewkes succeeding Richard Parsons as chief executive officer in 2008. And even NBC Universal, the struggling media unit of General Electric, appears to have some stability in its management ranks. Jeff Zucker, a veteran NBC Universal executive, was named as NBC Universal's new chairman and CEO in February 2007, replacing the retiring Bob Wright.

In addition, Murdoch seems so intent on keeping Chernin that he is even willing to give Chernin a higher annual compensation package than he himself earns. According to the company's fiscal 2007 proxy statement for shareholders, both Murdoch and Chernin earned an annual salary of $8.1 million. But after including stock awards, bonuses and other compensation, Chernin's total annual compensation package for fiscal 2007, which ended in June of that year, came out to nearly $34 million, ahead of $32.1 million for Murdoch.

What's more, Chernin's total compensation dwarfs that of other longtime News Corp. employees—not that either chief financial officer David DeVoe, who earned $11.7 million, or Ailes, who earned $10.9 million, has had any reason to complain.

But the fact that Chernin is the top moneymaker at News

Corp. has made it clear to Murdoch followers that Chernin has not only been an invaluable resource and adviser, but probably Rupert's most trusted lieutenant. While Murdoch is viewed as more hotheaded, Chernin has a reputation for being a calm negotiator.

Along those lines, Chernin has often tackled tough issues facing media companies with considerable aplomb. For example, he pleaded with the technology community in 2002 to help stop the illegal downloading of copyrighted content. During an address at the COMDEX technology trade show in Las Vegas in November of that year, he declared it was time for media conglomerates and tech companies to work together, and that doing so could be beneficial for both industries.

"The most powerful catalyst for growth is not piracy, but partnership," Chernin said. During his address, he pointed out how the tech industry could help the media business adapt and embrace change, pointing to the examples of the cable/satellite TV industry and the DVD industry, two new advances that media companies originally had their misgivings about. He argued that encrypted distribution of entertainment over the Internet would help advance consumer adoption of broadband Internet access and that this could have a major ripple effect throughout the technology sector, leading to more demand for servers, routers and software. "Both of our industries need to be seriously re-energized," Chernin said, speaking at a time when a sense of wariness was still felt in both Hollywood and Silicon Valley due to the dot-com meltdown a few years earlier.[15]

But even though Chernin may not be as gruff as his boss, he also showed that he can be tough as well during his COMDEX speech, constantly referring to free downloading of copyrighted music and videos as "looting," "piracy" and "digital hijacking," and joking that "if hundreds of thousands of dresses were stolen from Wal-Mart, the police would assemble a task force that would have Winona Ryder shaking in her boots."[16]

Chernin also showed some tough love when he stepped in during the Hollywood writers' strike in late 2007 and early 2008 to handle talks with the Writers Guild of America along with executives from other leading media companies. Chernin and Disney's Iger were widely credited for helping to bring about a resolution to a strike that crippled the television and movie industries after a work stoppage, which lasted a little more than fourteen weeks.

While Murdoch is often brusque and dismissive of criticism, Chernin is more of a goodwill ambassador. Speaking about the writers' strike at a Citigroup investment conference in January 2008, a month before the union and media companies reached an agreement, Chernin admitted that he and other studios would not roll over and accede to all the writers' demands, but he left the door open for fruitful talks.

"I take this strike very seriously. It is having a tremendous negative effect on people and not just the writers and not just those in the entertainment industry but a significant and serious economic impact on the city of Los Angeles," he said. "Conversely, I feel a responsibility not only to News Corp.

shareholders but the future of the industry to not make a deal that is economically indefensible. I wouldn't want to do things to hamper the industry. We believe, and frankly most other networks believe, that we can withstand a strike for a reasonably long time but we are anxious to figure out a viable solution for the industry."[17]

Murdoch, on the other hand, took a more antagonistic approach to the writers when discussing the strike in December 2007 in an interview on the Fox News Channel. Appearing on the network's *Your World with Neil Cavuto* show, he at first expressed hope that the strike would end soon, before launching into an attack on the union's characterization of News Corp. and other media companies.

"Now the rhetoric is, you know, big, fat companies and us poor writers, as though [they] want to change to some sort of socialist system and drag down the companies," Murdoch said.[18]

One can argue that the opposing personalities of Murdoch and Chernin, who is a registered Democrat, make for a textbook case of why having diverse opinions in a boardroom make for a better-managed company. If Chernin were simply a yes-man to Murdoch, would News Corp. be the leading media company it is today?

It's tough to definitively say, but it is worth pointing out that since Chernin became president and chief operating officer, Murdoch and News Corp. have avoided making the types of bold bets that could put the entire company's future at risk. News Corp. has not swapped more shares to investors that could try and take over the company down the road. The company has also steered clear of adding on mountains of debt to finance the Dow Jones deal and its expansion in digital media.

Still, would Murdoch agree, even if for only a limited period of time (while James Murdoch was gaining the seasoning to take over), to pass on control of the company to someone other than a Murdoch? Dorfman said he could envision a scenario in which Chernin is CEO, but it would only be temporary.

"Family is very important to Murdoch. No matter how many shareholders there are, he views News Corp. as a family enterprise. It's what he inherited from his father. I think he has made a decision to keep it in the family," said Dorfman. "If Murdoch were hit by a bus, the board would elevate Chernin on an interim business while they conducted a search, but ultimately James would succeed his father. If Chernin ever runs the company at the CEO level, it's simply until James is ready to take over."[19]

It is one thing for Murdoch to work closely with Chernin. Passing on the family legacy to him might be another matter, especially since Chernin has occasionally showed signs of not being in lockstep with his boss's thinking.

This is evident from Chernin's response to questions about the Dow Jones purchase. While Murdoch has often sounded like someone who won the lottery when discussing his newest acquisition, Chernin has taken a much more cautious approach when discussing Dow Jones and the impact it will have on News Corp.

Chernin, unlike Murdoch, was not brought up in the newspaper business. And it appears that he is not as enamored with newspapers as Murdoch is. At the Citigroup media conference in January 2008, Chernin bristled at the notion that News Corp. may have overpaid for Dow Jones and that the deal put the company's overall growth at risk.

"Let's put the purchase price in perspective. It's less than 10 percent of the market cap of the entire company. We're not sneezing at $5 billion, but people should not overstate the price relative to a company of our size. It's a mistake to look at this deal as doubling down on the newspaper business. We look at Dow Jones as the most valuable brand in financial services," Chernin said.[20]

But Chernin also is a staunch defender of News Corp.'s decision to spend aggressively in order to diversify geographically and enter new businesses. When asked if News Corp.—with seven different business lines spelled out in its financial statements—was an unwieldy conglomerate too difficult for investors to understand, Chernin quickly dismissed the question.

"I would argue that complexity is one of our greatest strengths. It allows us to make investments to grow the company and leads to our ability to make us significantly better positioned to withstand changes in the economy," Chernin said.[21]

Spoken like a true Murdoch. But will Rupert be able to overlook the fact that Chernin is not a Murdoch and pass the News Corp. leadership baton, albeit probably just for a brief period of time, to him until James Murdoch is deemed fully ready to take over the company? It could be a moot point, since Rupert shows no signs of slowing down; if he decides to stay on as chairman and CEO for another five years or so, James might be viewed as seasoned enough in the eyes of Wall Street so that a transition of power to James would not be considered premature.

Nonetheless, with Chernin's current employment contract set to expire in 2009, Murdoch faces a difficult decision. Does he extend Chernin's contract yet again or let him walk away, where presumably he would join another media rival in a leadership role and possibly do some competitive harm to News Corp.? If Rupert decides to sign Chernin to another contract, Wall Street could interpret that as a sign that he does not think James Murdoch is ready to take over as News Corp. CEO anytime soon and that Rupert wants to be able to tap Chernin as a safe pick to lead the company for a few years until James has the experience necessary to be granted the top spot.

It's also altogether possible that Chernin may not mind signing another contract with News Corp.—even if it was understood that he would never become the company's CEO—as long as Rupert was offering enough of a financial incentive to stay. Considering that Chernin has been the highest-compensated employee at News Corp. for most of the past decade, Murdoch might convince Chernin to stick around a few more years and perhaps even act as a mentor for James if the money continues to be right. Just as Murdoch has proven that he's willing to outbid other companies for assets that he craves, he has shown a willingness to do the same when it comes to people.

It's debatable whether Chernin, even as a CEO, would be able to pull in an annual compensation package in excess of $30 million at another media firm.

By way of comparison, Time Warner's Bewkes received $19.6 million in salary, bonuses, stock and other compensation in 2007. Disney's Iger received annual compensation of $27.7 million in 2007. Moonves's compensation package from CBS was worth nearly $37 million in 2007, but he signed a new four-year contract in 2007 that will tie his bonus to the company's performance, a move that could potentially lower his total compensation package drastically if CBS's ratings, revenue and profit growth slow. Viacom's Dauman received $20.6 million in compensation during 2006, his second year as Viacom CEO.

So Chernin may find it difficult to make as much money elsewhere as he does for News Corp. But if Rupert does sign Chernin to another contract, that could be viewed as a slap in James's face. By doing so Rupert would risk alienating his only adult child who is still working for News Corp. and who could be considered as a likely long-term successor. Given Murdoch's penchant for going against the grain and not necessarily caring about angering his company's investors, he could decide to cut ties with Chernin in 2009 and promote James to president and chief operating officer. That would be the boldest signal yet that Rupert thinks James is prepared to take over as CEO whenever that time may be, even should it be in the immediate future. One of the biggest knocks against James when he was tapped to head News Corp.'s European and Asian businesses in December 2007 was that he was just days away from his thirty-fifth birthday. But Rupert was only twenty-three years old when he took over the helm of the *Adelaide News* in 1954 following his father's death, and by the time Rupert was thirty-five in 1966 he had already acquired a television station in Australia, several more newspapers and had launched a national daily, the *Australian*.

Rupert won't live forever, no matter how much he may want to. He will soon need to make a decision, perhaps the biggest of his career, about his company's future. Chernin is probably the right choice as CEO for the short-term, but he is not, of course, Rupert's flesh and blood. James is waiting in the wings. And if for no other reason than fearing that James may also decide to leave News Corp., like Lachlan and Elisabeth, to start his own company if he perceives that he is being slighted by his father, Rupert may have no other choice but to strongly suggest to News Corp.'s board sometime within the next few years that James Murdoch be the new chairman and CEO of News Corp. Whether James will be able to do an effective job of running the News Corp. dynasty when the time comes is another question entirely.

EPILOGUE

The past few years have been a tumultuous time for Rupert Murdoch. He spent heavily in order to transform News Corp. from a company with very few top Internet media properties to one of the leading players on the digital landscape. But it's uncertain whether he bet on the right digital horse, as some fear that MySpace's popularity may already have peaked. What's more, Murdoch's reported interest in forming a joint venture with Yahoo for a mere minority stake in the combined company may be a sign that he has already grown bored with the Internet. It looks like Murdoch's attention is no longer focused on the Web, although it was all he could focus on in 2005 and early 2006.

Murdoch has quickly latched on to a new fixation: owning Dow Jones and the *Wall Street Journal*. Former News Corp. employee Andrew Neil said in his January 2008 testimony to a House of Lords committee looking at media ownership in Britain that Murdoch "has now of course got a new toy which totally obsesses him which is the *Wall Street Journal* and he does not want to talk about anything else."[1]

But for how long will this be the case? Will Murdoch soon tire of Dow Jones and find something else to focus his waking moments on? After all, before Dow Jones and the Internet, Murdoch was fixated on owning a presence in the U.S. satellite television market and he only wound up owning a piece of DirecTV for a little more than three years before he decided to sell it.

In the latter stages of 2007 and early part of 2008, Wall Street was punishing media companies for their exposure to the advertising market at a time when the United States appeared to be heading for recession and was threatening to take the global economy along with it. In retrospect, paying a 65 percent premium for Dow Jones may not have been the smart thing to do, considering that many analysts believed even online advertising spending would not be immune to an economic slowdown. What's more, the decision to launch a financial news cable network in the face of an economic and stock market slump also did not bode well for News Corp.

Has Murdoch lost that Midas touch for media? Is it time for him to move on? For what it's worth, longtime investors still have no major reason to complain about Murdoch. His acumen for making the right deals at the right time, even if they did involve overpaying a bit, has served those who have backed Murdoch over the long haul quite well.

Since News Corp.'s stock first began trading on the New York Stock Exchange in 1986, shares have gained more than 1,000 percent. The stock has outperformed the Dow Jones Industrial Average, S&P 500 and NASDAQ Composite during that time frame but has lagged rival Walt Disney.

And even though Murdoch has often irritated shareholders in the past by making similar mistakes over and over again, especially when he lets his ego get in the way of common financial sense, it seems that as Murdoch has gotten older, he truly has become wiser as well. Maybe he has mellowed and is less inclined to make huge gambles. Perhaps he is allowing Chernin more of a say. If that's true, Chernin may be convincing Murdoch to be more fiscally conservative with News Corp.'s money. Whatever the reason, Murdoch does not seem to be making the "bet the ranch"–type moves that often had put News Corp. in jeopardy in the past.

Murdoch has never been afraid to grow News Corp. through acquisitions. But the company has scaled back in recent years in some businesses even as it has made big acquisitions in others. In June 2007, the company announced it was seeking "strategic options"—Wall Street's euphemism for putting something up for sale—for News Outdoor Group, a subsidiary that owns and operates billboards in emerging markets such as Russia and other countries in Eastern Europe as well as Turkey, Israel, India and countries in Southeast Asia. As of early 2008, there was no update on a sale of the group.

But News Corp. also put several of its small local television stations on the block in June 2007. They found a buyer by year's end. The company also announced it had agreed to sell eight Fox-affiliated stations in markets including Cleveland, Denver and St. Louis to Oak Hill Capital Partners, a private equity firm, for $1.1 billion in cash. The deal closed during the third quarter of 2008.

So even if News Corp. has its sights set on another large deal, there is a growing sense that News Corp. now has the balance-sheet flexibility to be more acquisitive. In fact, some analysts speculate that the company could have made a play for the Weather Channel, a cable network that privately held Landmark Communications announced was for sale in January 2008. General Electric–owned NBC Universal and two private-equity investment firms agreed in July 2008 to buy the Weather Channel for $3.5 billion. Thus, a purchase would have cost News Corp. several billion dollars, but analysts were not concerned that News Corp. would have to raise a significant amount of debt to finance a deal. That's a far cry from the late 1980s and early 1990s, when Murdoch spent heavily and in order to avoid bankruptcy was ultimately forced to sell off many of the assets he had bought.

Yet, Murdoch is ever the acquirer. As long as there are companies willing to sell, it seems likely that he is willing to take a look at the books. Building through acquisition is simply an old habit that proves hard, if not impossible, for Murdoch to break.

"We have no big lumps of debt to pay off. We are very secure where we are even though we don't have a lot of cash now that we paid $5 billion for Dow Jones," Murdoch said in March 2008. "We are not on the hunt for big multibillion-dollar things but we think everything will get cheaper by the way. So we may get tempted to do some small things."[2]

But Dave Novosel, an analyst with Gimme Credit, an independent research firm in New York that analyzes corporate debt, wrote in a report in January 2008 that News Corp. would likely have been able to offer as much as $5 billion for the Weather Channel without having to significantly raise its debt load.

Novosel pointed out that News Corp. has done a better job of identifying businesses that are no longer part of the company's core strength and unloading them, specifically citing the eight TV stations sold to Oak Hill as evidence that Murdoch is no longer just a serial acquirer.

"News Corp. is not only willing to add assets, but it will cull those properties that have lesser potential. For example, the divested TV stations were in markets where the opportunity to expand profitability was muted," Novosel wrote. Novosel even suggested that News Corp. could consider selling Harper-Collins, since the publishing unit only accounts for about 5 percent of total revenues and has been a slow grower for News Corp. Novosel estimated that HarperCollins could be worth $1.2 billion to $1.4 billion in a sale.

Unloading HarperCollins may not be something that Murdoch would like to do for sentimental reasons. He has owned the book publisher since buying Harper & Row in 1987. But as Novosel pointed out, HarperCollins has hardly been a star for News Corp. as of late. In fiscal 2007, revenues at HarperCollins rose just 3 percent while operating profits fell 5 percent. Conditions did not improve during the first three quarters of fiscal 2008 as HarperCollins' revenues fell another 1 percent and operating profits declined by 4 percent from the same period a year earlier. And HarperCollins' longtime chief executive officer, Jane Friedman, suddenly resigned in June 2008.

What's more, HarperCollins has been a public relations nightmare for Murdoch in the past few years. The memory of the fiasco over the canceled Chris Patten memoir about China back in 1998—HarperCollins killed a book written by the former governor of Hong Kong that was critical of the communist regime in Beijing—has been still fresh in the minds of many in the book industry. But this paled in comparison to the uproar that took place when it was learned that Judith Regan, a high-profile editor with her own imprint at HarperCollins, was planning to publish a book written by former NFL football star O. J. Simpson about the murder of his ex-wife Nicole Brown-Simpson and her friend Ron Goldman.

Simpson was accused of the 1994 murders, but, following a sensational trial in 1995, he was acquitted. Simpson later was found liable for Brown-Simpson and Goldman's deaths in a civil trial in 1997. Simpson has remained a public curiosity ever since, and in 2006 HarperCollins agreed to publish *If I Did It*, a fictional account by Simpson about how he would have committed the murders. A television special to promote the book was also set to air on Fox, adding to the public outcry against News Corp.

On November 20, 2006, News Corp. pulled the plug on both the book and the special. An embarrassed Murdoch said in a statement that he and other members of News Corp.'s senior management "agree with the American public that this was an ill-considered project. We are sorry for any pain this has caused the families of Ron Goldman and Nicole Brown-Simpson."[3]

The spotlight intensified on HarperCollins, however, after another Regan book also received negative attention. In December 2006, it was reported that Regan was planning to publish a "fictional biography" of beloved New York Yankees legend Mickey Mantle, which, among other things, alleged he was having an affair with Marilyn Monroe at the time the starlet was dating future husband and Mantle teammate Joe DiMaggio.

Regan was fired by HarperCollins in December 2006 for allegedly using anti-Semitic remarks in a phone conversation with a HarperCollins lawyer. Regan later claimed in a November 2007 defamation lawsuit against News Corp. that the real reason she was fired was because her affair with Bernard Kerik, who was the New York City police commissioner under Mayor Rudolph Giuliani at the time of the September 11, 2001, terrorist attacks, might hurt Giuliani's bid for the presidency. She alleged that News Corp. was concerned about information she may have had about Kerik, who was indicted on corruption charges in November 2007. Regan accused News Corp. of creating a "smear campaign" to destroy her reputation.

"The smear campaign was necessary to advance News Corp.'s political agenda, which has long centered on protecting Rudy Giuliani's presidential ambitions," Regan said in her complaint.[4]

News Corp. and Regan announced in January 2008 that the two parties had reached a confidential settlement of the lawsuit, with neither News Corp. nor Regan admitting any liability. In a statement, News Corp. indicated that "after carefully considering the matter, we accept Ms. Regan's position that she did not say anything that was anti-Semitic in nature, and further believe that Ms. Regan is not anti-Semitic," and added that "Ms. Regan is a talented publisher who created many award-winning and bestselling books during her twelve and a half years at the company. News Corp. thanks Ms. Regan for her outstanding contributions and wishes her continued success."[5]

Speaking about Regan at the McGraw-Hill media conference in February 2007, Murdoch said he regretted losing touch with her on the decisions about the Simpson book but added that "she was not a team player. That's putting it mildly."[6]

It certainly sounds like Murdoch is no longer as enamored with book publishing as he once was. So with that in mind, it would not be a huge shock to see HarperCollins eventually fall the way of DirecTV, *TV Guide* and the Los Angeles Dodgers as

Murdoch, or a successor, may come to the realization that the division does not mesh well with other more rapidly growing assets.

"If you look at the big media companies, they are all going through a reevaluation of the conglomerate model. It may not make as much sense to own everything," said Glover Lawrence, cofounder of McNamee Lawrence & Company, an investment bank based in Boston, about the possibility of a HarperCollins sale shortly after Regan was fired. "Book publishers are generally very cash flow predictable so they make ideal targets for private equity buyers."[7]

Then again, there had been chatter that News Corp. might sell HarperCollins before the Regan/Simpson debacle. Earlier in 2006, Time Warner sold its book unit to French media firm Lagardère, raising speculation that News Corp. might follow suit and exit the book business.

"A lot of times when one media company takes the lead like that, others come to similar conclusions," said media investment banker Reed Phillips in December 2006. But he added that he wasn't sure Murdoch necessarily wanted to get rid of HarperCollins, since he thought that "now that they've dismissed Regan, their view probably would be problem solved. I don't think they would necessarily believe it would now be the time to sell HarperCollins," he said.[8]

What's more, the deterioration in the credit markets in 2007 and 2008 has made it much less likely that a private equity firm would be interested in making, or be able to make, a deal for HarperCollins.

Regardless of whether Murdoch eventually looks to shed more assets or not, it is clear that he is not going to sit idly by as the media landscape changes. Media experts anticipate more deals from News Corp. to come even if they're not sure what exactly will be Murdoch's next target.

"This is a potent combination of assets put together by Murdoch. There are attackers and there are defenders. Murdoch is an attacker," said John Suhler, a founding general partner and president of Veronis Suhler Stevenson, a New York–based private equity firm that focuses mainly on media deals, in October 2007.[9]

Murdoch himself has suggested that he's always looking for other merger targets. During a News Corp. earnings conference call in August 2006, he said that "we'd buy anything if the price is right,"[10] and during the Goldman Sachs media conference in September 2007 he coyly said that "we have competitors with desirable assets but as far as I'm concerned they are not selling them."[11]

But one thing seems certain: even if Murdoch does want to strike more deals, it appears that he's learned the hard way never to let another investor acquire too much of a stake in News Corp. Murdoch has always been somewhat reluctant to use News Corp. stock as acquisition currency, but he has grown even more wary of doing so following the confrontation with Malone.

Now that Malone's Liberty Media has exchanged its stake in News Corp. for News Corp.'s DirecTV holdings, the second-largest shareholder of News Corp. after the Murdoch family is mutual fund firm Dodge & Cox—which mainly owns Class A shares with limited voting power. The second-largest voting shareholder is Saudi Prince Al-Waleed bin Talal, the billionaire most famous for helping to bail out banking giant Citicorp in the 1990s by investing in the company. The bank is now known as Citigroup and Prince Al-Waleed is Citigroup's biggest investor.

So Murdoch may continue to buy and sell assets, but he's not likely to make the mistake of giving up control of a large chunk of his company's shares to an outsider ever again. "He wants to do deals but he doesn't want to be using stock all that much," said Dorfman.[12]

Dorfman adds that he believes Murdoch will never stop hunting for more things to buy. But it may be tough for him to make many more acquisitions until credit markets improve if he wants to use cash and debt, as opposed to News Corp. shares. This could wind up being a good thing for News Corp. shareholders, however, as it may force Murdoch to take a breather after the Dow Jones deal.

"His thirst for acquisitions will be difficult to quench given the current credit markets," Dorfman said. "But the company is now financially sound. I don't believe that he's got as much of an issue of the balance sheet being a house of cards falling down like it was in the 1980s. For the time being, this may be fortuitous. It may give Murdoch the opportunity to consolidate and integrate Dow Jones."[13]

Another potential piece of good news for shareholders is that Murdoch has appeared to take some of the criticism of himself to heart. Whether it is fear that a continued backlash would hurt his company's financial standing around the world or that he's truly softened in the past few years is an open question. But there is no denying that News Corp. has taken steps in the past few years to appear a little more "fair and balanced."

For example, HarperCollins published *At the Center of the Storm*, a best-selling memoir by ex-CIA director George Tenet that was highly critical of the war in Iraq and Vice President Dick Cheney in April 2007. And in 2006, William Morrow, an imprint of HarperCollins, published a book by Joe Maguire called *Brainless: The Lies and Lunacy of Ann Coulter*.

Murdoch has also shown glimpses, albeit brief, of not taking himself too seriously in the past few years—or at least of being able to tolerate the perception of him as a meddlesome media mogul. The long-running animated hit *The Simpsons* has routinely poked fun at Murdoch during the show's run on Fox and has stepped up its criticism of him and News Corp. in the past few years. Most recently, the overly pious character Ned Flanders referred to the *Wall Street Journal* in the show's traditional Halloween episode in November 2007 this way:

"I just wanna say that for those watching this network, you're all going to hell and that includes FX, Fox Sports, and our newest devil's portal, the *Wall Street Journal*. Welcome to the club!"

Whether Murdoch decides it is time to call it quits and enjoy the fruits of the media empire he has built remains to be seen. But those who have followed him closely doubt that he will ever relinquish the desire to finish ahead of the competition. Murdoch may have mellowed, but it's unlikely he will ever completely change.

"I would never underestimate Rupert Murdoch's willingness to win. He's going to do what he needs to do to win," said Bill Carroll, vice president and director of programming with Katz Television Group, a media buying and consulting firm based in New York, in 2006.[14]

But what it all boils down to, what seems to motivate nearly every one of Murdoch's business decisions—from the most mundane to the boldest and most controversial—is his insatiable desire to demonstrate that those who doubt him are wrong and to defy conventional wisdom. And what greater challenge could there be for Murdoch than to do battle with the notions of time and age? At this point in his career, the only thing he may have left to prove is that he can still function as a competent chairman and CEO for far longer than anyone would have thought imaginable. So don't be surprised to see Murdoch still lurking around the News Corp. executive suite well into his eighties or even nineties. There probably would be no greater delight for Murdoch than sticking around long enough to give Chloe and Grace their first jobs at News Corp.

ACKNOWLEDGMENTS

There are many people to thank for helping me survive this process with my sanity (largely) intact. First and foremost, Jeffrey Krames at Portfolio deserves a ton of praise and my undying gratitude for approaching me with the idea to write this book in the first place. I truly appreciate his faith in me, particularly since this is my first book. His guidance and careful editing of the manuscript were indispensable. I would also like to thank Jillian Gray at Portfolio for providing me with many wonderful suggestions on the manuscript and for helping guide me through the book writing and publishing process in general.

At CNNMoney.com, the patience and support of several of my editors, most notably Chris Peacock, Lex Haris, Rich Barbieri and Mark Meinero, was crucial. Thanks for putting up with my ever-mounting stress levels while I simultaneously juggled the writing of this book with my responsibilities on the job. Jim

Ledbetter, a former colleague of mine at CNNMoney.com, was also instrumental in the success of this book, as he edited much of my coverage of News Corp. and Murdoch over the past few years. Thanks, Jim, for always steering me on the right track.

Many of the sources for this book proved to be invaluable. Thanks in particular to Richard Dorfman, Larry Haverty, Alan Gould, Laura Martin and David Joyce for their expert opinions about Murdoch and the media industry and their willingness to share them with me over the past few years.

My family, particularly my brother Steve and my father Dick, have also always been there for me and I appreciate that. But most of all, I'd like to thank my wife, Beth, for being my constant champion, confidante and source of reason and perspective during times when I doubted myself. Thanks also for acting as my "agent." Beth, I love you so much, and this book would not have been possible without you.

NOTES

Introduction

1. McGraw-Hill Media Summit, New York, February 8, 2007.
2. Paul R. La Monica, "Don't Believe the MySpace Hype," CNNMoney .com, June 7, 2006, http://money.cnn.com/2006/06/07/commen tary/mediabiz/index.htm.
3. Goldman Sachs' Communacopia XVI Conference, New York, September 18, 2007.
4. The Future of Business Media Conference, New York, October 30, 2007.
5. Ibid.
6. Jacques Steinberg and Brian Stelter, "Few Viewers for Infancy of Fox Business," *New York Times*, January 4, 2008.
7. Tim Arango, "Inside Fox Business News," *Fortune*, October 15, 2007.
8. Paul R. La Monica, "Don't Bet on a 'Paper' Chase," CNNMoney.com, August 2, 2007, http://money.cnn.com/2007/08/02/news/compa nies/newspaper_mergers/index.htm.
9. Conversation with the author, June 7, 2007.

Chapter 1: Start Spreading the News

1. Conversation with the author, March 6, 2008.
2. House of Lords Select Committee on Communications testimony, January 16, 2008, http://www.publications.parliament.uk/pa/ld /lduncorr/comms160108ev8.pdf.
3. Ibid.
4. Conversation with the author, March 6, 2008.
5. House of Lords Select Committee on Communications testimony, September 17, 2007, http://www.parliament.uk/parliamentary_com mittees/communications.cfm.
6. Ibid.
7. Ibid.
8. House of Lords Select Committee on Communications testimony, January 16, 2008, http://www.publications.parliament.uk/pa/ld /lduncorr/comms160108ev8.pdf.
9. Ibid.
10. Ibid.
11. Ibid.
12. House of Lords Select Committee on Communications testimony, January 23, 2008, http://www.publications.parliament.uk/pa/ld /lduncorr/comms230108ev15.pdf.
13. Ibid.
14. Ibid.
15. Ibid.
16. House of Lords Select Committee on Communications testimony, January 16, 2008, http://www.publications.parliament.uk/pa/ld /lduncorr/comms160108ev8.pdf.
17. House of Lords Select Committee on Communications testimony, January 23, 2008, http://www.publications.parliament.uk/pa/ld /lduncorr/comms230108ev15.pdf.
18. Ibid.
19. Ibid.

20. House of Lords Select Committee on Communications testimony, September 17, 2007, http://www.parliament.uk/parliamentary_com mittees/communications.cfm.

21. Paul R. La Monica, "Don't Bet on a 'Paper' Chase," CNNMoney.com, August 2, 2007, http://money.cnn.com/2007/08/02/news/compa nies/newspaper_mergers/index.htm.

22. The Future of Business Media Conference, New York, October 30, 2007.

23. http://www.newscorp.com/news/news_285.html.

24. Ibid.

25. Paul R. La Monica, "Don't Bet on a 'Paper' Chase," CNNMoney.com, August 2, 2007, http://money.cnn.com/2007/08/02/news/compa nies/newspaper_mergers/index.htm.

26. http://www.newscorp.com/news/news_222.html.

27. Paul R. La Monica, "Good News for Newspaper Stocks?" CNNMoney .com, September 26, 2007, http://mediabiz.blogs.cnnmoney.cnn .com/2007/09/26/good-news-for-newspaper-stocks/.

28. http://www.newscorp.com/news/news_316.html.

29. Paul R. La Monica, "Good News for Newspaper Stocks?" CNNMoney .com, September 26, 2007, http://mediabiz.blogs.cnnmoney.cnn .com/2007/09/26/good-news-for-newspaper-stocks/.

Chapter 2: Crazy Like a Fox

1. Richard W. Stevenson, "Murdoch Is Buying 50% of Fox," *New York Times*, March 21, 1985.

2. Michael Schrage, "TV Stations Pose Risk for Murdoch," *Washington Post*, May 19, 1985.

3. Ibid.

4. Ibid.

5. " 'What's Next?'—Rupert Murdoch Acquires Ziff-Davis' Business Magazines," *Folio: The Magazine for Magazine Management*, May 1985.

6. P. J. Bednarski, "Murdoch Plans Fourth Network," *Chicago Sun-Times*, October 10, 1985.

7. "Murdoch Lays Plan for 4th TV Network," *Los Angeles Times*, October 10, 1985.

8. Roger Gillott, "Fox TV Network Could Take Decades to Build, Analysts Say," Associated Press, October 10, 1985.

9. Ibid.

10. Michael Collins, "Murdoch Outlines Plans for 4th Network," United Press International, January 5, 1986.

11. Paul R. La Monica, "MyNetworkTV: Crazy Like a . . . ," CNNMoney .com, February 23, 2006, http://money.cnn.com/2006/02/23/news /companies/mynetworktv/index.htm.

12. http://www.newscorp.com/news/news_267.html.

13. Paul R. La Monica, "Murdoch Unveils MySpace Ambitions," CNN Money.com, September 19, 2006, http://money.cnn.com/2006 /09/19/technology/myspace/index.htm.

14. http://www.newscorp.com/news/Murdoch_testimony_5_8_03 .pdf.

15. http://www.newscorp.com/news/news_247.html.

16. Conversation with the author, March 6, 2008.

17. Jane Martinson, "Billionaire Dropout Still Creates by the Seat of His Pants," *Guardian*, October 27, 2006.

Chapter 3: Hooked on Cable

1. http://www.newscorp.com/news/news_247.html.

2. Steve McClellan, "Ailes Heads Fox Cable News Channel," *Broadcasting and Cable*, February 5, 1996.

3. Ibid.

4. Bill Carter, "Murdoch Joins a Cable-TV Rush into the Crowded All-News Field," *New York Times*, January 31, 1996.

5. Ibid.

6. Charles Haddad, "Observers Question Murdoch's 24-Hour News Plan," *Atlanta-Journal Constitution*, January 31, 1996.

7. Wayne Walley, "Fox Takes 24-Hour Cable News Plunge," *Electronic Media*, February 5, 1996.

8. Ibid.

9. Howard Rosenberg, "Cutting Across the Bias of the Fox News Channel," *Los Angeles Times*, October 11, 1996.

10. Ibid.

11. Ibid.

12. Howard Kurtz, "Is Fox's News Channel Cable-Ready?" *Washington Post*, October 14, 1996.

13. Manuel Mendoza, "Don't Worry Yet, CNN," *Dallas Morning News*, October 8, 1996.

14. Pete Schulberg, "Fox News Channel Off to Quick, Edgy Start," *Oregonian*, October 9, 1996.

15. Howard Kurtz, "Is Fox's News Channel Cable-Ready?" *Washington Post*, October 14, 1996.

16. Ibid.

17. David Usborne, "Murdoch Meets His Match," *Independent*, November 24, 1996.

18. Ibid.

19. Nancy Dunne, "Murdoch Lashes Media Rival," *Financial Times*, February 27, 1996.

20. David Usborne, "Murdoch Meets His Match," *Independent*, November 24, 1996.

21. Ibid.

22. Ibid.

23. http://www.adl.org/PresRele/HolNa_52/2828_52.asp.

24. David Usborne, "Murdoch Meets His Match," *Independent*, November 24, 1996.

25. "The Most Anticipated Bout of 1997: Murdoch vs. Turner," *Daily News* (L.A.), June 22, 1997.

26. Ibid.

27. Jill Goldsmith, "Rupe's Remarks Irk Peacock, Time Warner," *Variety*, November 1999.

28. http://www.newscorp.com/news/news_350.html.

29. http://www.newscorp.com/news/news_226.html.

30. Marvin Kitman, "Murdoch May Finally Get His News," *Newsday*, February 5, 1996.

31. House of Lords Select Committee on Communications testimony, September 17, 2007, http://www.parliament.uk/parliamentary_committees/communications.cfm.

32. Ibid.

33. Ibid.

34. http://www.newscorp.com/news/news_350.html.

35. Ibid.

36. Paul R. La Monica, "Getting Down to (Fox) Business," CNNMoney.com, October 15, 2007, http://mediabiz.blogs.cnnmoney.cnn.com/2007/10/15/getting-down-to-fox-business/.

37. Ibid.

38. Bear Stearns Media Conference, Palm Beach, Florida, March 10, 2008.

39. Ibid.

40. http://www.newscorp.com/news/news_350.html.

Chapter 4: The Sky's the Limit

1. Conversation with the author, October 1, 2007.

2. Raymond Snoddy, "Call Halted Murdoch Deal," *Times* (London), March 27, 1998.

3. http://phx.corporate-ir.net/phoenix.zhtml?c=104016&p=irol-newsArticle_Print&ID=144647&highlight=manchester.

4. http://www.newscorp.com/news/news_175.html.

5. http://www.newscorp.com/news/news_197.html.

6. Ibid.

7. http://www.newscorp.com/news/news_361.html.

8. Rupert Murdoch, "The New Freedom," *Herald Sun,* September 3, 1993.

9. Eric Alterman, "Think Again. The Complicated Corruptions of Rupert Murdoch and the *Wall Street Journal,*" May 24, 2007, http://www.amer icanprogress.org/issues/2007/05/complicated_corruptions.html.

10. Eric Pooley, "Rupert Murdoch Speaks," *Time,* June 28, 2007, http://www.time.com/time/business/article/0,8599,1638182,00.html.

11. Mark Riley, "What Culture? Murdoch Deems Tibet Is Better Off Under China," *Sydney Morning Herald*, September 8, 1999.

12. Ibid.

13. http://www.newscorp.com/news/news_321.html.

14. Eric Boehlert, "Pimping for the People's Republic," Salon.com, March 30, 2001, http://archive.salon.com/news/feature/2001/03/30/china /print.html.

15. http://www.newscorp.com/news/news_355.html.

16. Donald Greenlees, "Dow Jones Editor Gets 'Cold Feet' on a Critique of Murdoch," *International Herald Tribune,* February 28, 2008.

17. Ibid.

18. Conversation with the author, March 6, 2008.

19. http://www.newscorp.com/news/news_321.html.

20. Ibid.

21. Ibid.

22. Ibid.

23. Ibid.

Chapter 5: Wheeling and Dealing

1. Paul R. La Monica. "Murdoch Still Hearts Newspapers." CNNMoney .com. September 18, 2007, http://mediabiz.blogs.cnnmoney.cnn .com/2007/09/18/murdoch-still-hearts-newspapers/.

2. Paul R. La Monica, "Start Spreading the News (Corp.)," CNNMoney .com, April 2, 2007, http://money.cnn.com/2007/04/02/news/com panies/newscorp/index.htm.

3. Paul R. La Monica, "Icahn Calls for Time Warner Breakup, Buyback," CNNMoney.com, February 7, 2006, http://money.cnn.com/2006 /02/07/news/companies/timewarner_icahn/index.htm.

4. Conversation with the author, July 20, 2006.

5. Ibid.

6. Paul R. La Monica, "Rupert Murdoch's Secret TiVo," CNNMoney.com, February 2, 2007, http://money.cnn.com/2007/02/02/news/compa nies/nds/index.htm.

7. Conversation with the author, March 6, 2008.

8. Citigroup Eighteenth Annual Entertainment, Media and Telecommu- nications Conference, Phoenix, Arizona, January 9, 2008.

9. "Murdoch, Malone to Swap," CNNMoney.com, September 27, 2000, http://money.cnn.com/2000/09/27/deals/murdoch_malone/in dex.htm.

10. Ronald Grover, Tom Lowry and Larry Armstrong, "Henry Yuen: TV Guy," *BusinessWeek*, March 12, 2001.

11. Conversation with the author, July 10, 2007.

12. Bryan Firth, "King of Cable's Purchase Endorses News," *Australian,* April 7, 1999.

13. http://www.newscorp.com/news/news_188.html.

14. Ibid.

15. Ibid.

16. http://www.newscorp.com/news/news_197.html.

17. http://www.newscorp.com/news/Murdoch_testimony_5_8_03.pdf.

18. Conversation with the author, March 15, 2006.

19. http://phx.corporate-ir.net/phoenix.zhtml?c=61138&p=irol-news Article&ID=706832&highlight=.

20. Tim Burt, "Liberty's Malone in News Corp. Talks," *Financial Times*, April 19, 2004.

21. http://www.newscorp.com/news/news_230.html.

22. http://www.newscorp.com/news/news_322.html.

23. http://phx.corporate-ir.net/phoenix.zhtml?c=61138&p=irol-news Article&ID=944564&highlight=.

24. McGraw-Hill Media Summit, New York, February 8, 2007.

25. Ibid.

26. Paul R. La Monica, "News Corp. Is Out-Foxing Its Media Rivals," CNNMoney.com, April 2, 2007, http://money.cnn.com/2007/04 /02/news/companies/newscorp/index.htm.

27. Paul R. La Monica, "Rupert Murdoch's Secret TiVo," CNNMoney.com, February 2, 2007.

28. Ibid.

29. Ibid.

Chapter 6: Rupert 2.0

1. McGraw-Hill Media Summit, New York, February 8, 2007.

2. Fortune Brainstorm Conference, Aspen, Colorado, June 30, 2006.

3. Ibid.

4. http://www.newscorp.com/news/news_250.html.

5. http://www.newscorp.com/news/news_251.html.

6. Paul R. La Monica, "21st Century Fox," CNNMoney.com, August 22, 2005, http://money.cnn.com/2005/08/22/news/fortune500/mur doch/index.htm.

7. http://www.newscorp.com/news/news_259.html.

8. Paul R. La Monica, "Do 'You' Really Matter?" CNNMoney.com, January 17, 2007, http://money.cnn.com/2007/01/17/commentary/medi abiz/index.htm.

9. http://www.newscorp.com/news/news_267.html.

10. Paul R. La Monica, "Move Over, MySpace," CNNMoney.com, March 19, 2007, http://money.cnn.com/2007/03/19/news/companies/social networks/index.htm.

11. Fortune Brainstorm Conference, Aspen, Colorado, June 30, 2006.

12. Ibid.

13. McGraw-Hill Media Summit, New York, February 8, 2007.
14. Paul R. La Monica, "Murdoch Gives Dow Jones the Page Six Treatment," CNNMoney.com, August 8, 2007, http://mediabiz.blogs .cnnmoney.cnn.com/2007/08/08/murdoch-gives-dow-jones-the -page-six-treatment/.
15. McGraw-Hill Media Summit, New York, February 8, 2007.
16. Conversation with the author. November 3, 2006.
17. Peter Kafka, "Google: MySpace Deal Hurting Us," *Silicon Alley Insider*, February 1, 2008, http://www.alleyinsider.com/2008/2/google _myspace_deal_hurting_us_nws.
18. Ibid.
19. Personal notes from conference call, February 4, 2008.
20. Bear Stearns Media Conference, Palm Beach, Florida, March 10, 2008.
21. McGraw-Hill Media Summit, New York, February 8, 2007.
22. Bear Stearns Media Conference, Palm Beach, Florida, March 10, 2008.
23. Paul R. La Monica, "Don't Believe the MySpace Hype," CNNMoney .com, June 7, 2006.
24. McGraw-Hill Media Summit, New York, February 8, 2007.
25. Paul R. La Monica, "Murdoch Still Hearts Newspapers," CNNMoney .com, September 18, 2007.
26. Ibid.
27. Paul R. La Monica, "No Rally for Media Stocks," CNNMoney.com, October 1, 2007, http://mediabiz.blogs.cnnmoney.cnn.com/2007/10 /01/no-rally-for-media-stocks/.
28. Personal notes from conference call, August 8, 2006.
29. Personal notes from conference call, February 4, 2008.
30. Bear Stearns Media Conference, Palm Beach, Florida, March 10, 2008.
31. Ibid.

Chapter 7: The Battle for Dow Jones

1. Peter Preston, "Distinguished Newspaper Title for Sale. Do I Hear Any Bids?" *Observer*, June 26, 2005.

2. McGraw-Hill Media Summit, New York, February 8, 2007.

3. David Yelland, "What Would Rupert Give for the *FT*?" *Evening Standard*, August 11, 2004.

4. Ibid.

5. Notes from News Corp. conference call, May 9, 2007.

6. Ibid.

7. http://www.iape1096.org/news/2007/01_newscorp.php.

8. Paul R. La Monica, "Dow Jones: The Lamest Bidding War Ever," CNNMoney.com, June 7, 2007, http://mediabiz.blogs.cnnmoney.cnn .com/2007/06/07/dow-jones-the-lamest-bidding-war-ever/.

9. Paul R. La Monica, "Murdoch's Bold Bid for the *Journal*," CNNMoney .com, May 1, 2007, http://money.cnn.com/2007/05/01/news/compa nies/newspapers/index.htm.

10. Ibid.

11. Paul R. La Monica, "GE Doesn't Need Microsoft to Buy Dow Jones," CNNMoney.com, June 11, 2007, http://mediabiz.blogs.cnnmoney.cnn .com/2007/06/11/ge-doesnt-need-microsoft-to-buy-dow-jones/.

12. Paul R. La Monica, "Dow Jones Deal Dead? Don't Bet on It," CNNMoney.com, July 30, 2007, http://mediabiz.blogs.cnnmoney .cnn.com/2007/07/30/dow-jones-deal-dead-dont-bet-on-it/.

13. Ibid.

14. Paul R. La Monica, "Dow Jones: The Lamest Bidding War Ever," CNNMoney.com, June 7, 2007, http://mediabiz.blogs.cnnmoney.cnn .com/2007/06/07/dow-jones-the-lamest-bidding-war-ever/.

15. Paul R. La Monica, "WSJ Reporters Get a Case of Blue Flu," CNNMoney.com, June 28, 2007, http://mediabiz.blogs.cnnmoney .cnn.com/2007/06/28/wsj-reporters-get-a-case-of-blue-flu/.

16. Ibid.

17. Eric Pooley, "Rupert Murdoch Speaks," *Time*, June 28, 2007.

18. Paul R. La Monica, "Murdoch Gets Closer to Winning Dow Jones," CNNMoney.com, June 25, 2007, http://mediabiz.blogs.cnnmoney .cnn.com/2007/06/25/murdoch-gets-closer-to-winning-dow -jones/.

19. Paul R. La Monica, "Dow Jones Deal Dead? Don't Bet on It," CNNMoney.com, July 30, 2007, http://mediabiz.blogs.cnnmoney.cnn.com/2007/07/30/dow-jones-deal-dead-dont-bet-on-it/.

20. Ibid.

21. http://www.newscorp.com/news/news_347.html.

22. Ibid.

23. Ibid.

24. Goldman Sachs' Communacopia XVI Conference, New York, September 18, 2007.

25. Paul R. La Monica, "Murdoch Gives Dow Jones the Page Six Treatment," CNNMoney.com, August 8, 2007, http://mediabiz.blogs.cnnmoney.cnn.com/2007/08/08/murdoch-gives-dow-jones-the-page-six-treatment/.

26. Paul R. La Monica, "News Corp. Wins Fight for Dow Jones," CNNMoney.com, July 31, 2007, http://money.cnn.com/2007/07/31/news/companies/dowjones_newscorp/index.htm.

27. Paul R. La Monica, "Rupert Buying Dow Jones Bad for Democracy?" CNNMoney.com, July 18, 2007, http://mediabiz.blogs.cnnmoney.cnn.com/2007/07/18/rupert-buying-dow-jones-bad-for-democracy/.

28. Ibid.

29. Paul R. La Monica, "News Corp. Wins Fight for Dow Jones," CNNMoney.com, July 31, 2007, http://money.cnn.com/2007/07/31/news/companies/dowjones_newscorp/index.htm.

30. Ibid.

31. Paul R. La Monica, "Murdoch Gives Dow Jones the Page Six Treatment," CNNMoney.com, August 8, 2007, http://mediabiz.blogs.cnnmoney.cnn.com/2007/08/08/murdoch-gives-dow-jones-the-page-six-treatment/.

32. Ibid.

33. Goldman Sachs' Communacopia XVI Conference, New York, September 18, 2007.

34. Notes from News Corp. conference call, February 4, 2008.

35. Ibid.

36. Bear Stearns Media Conference, Palm Beach, Florida, March 10, 2008.

37. http://www.newscorp.com/news/news_354.html.

38. http://www.newscorp.com/news/news_356.html.

39. Paul R. La Monica, "Murdoch: 'Crazy Like a Fox' or Just Crazy?" CNNMoney.com, July 26, 2007, http://mediabiz.blogs.cnnmoney.cnn.com/2007/06/26/murdoch-crazy-like-a-fox-or-just-crazy/.

40. Ibid.

41. Ibid.

42. Paul R. La Monica, "The Rupert Discount," CNNMoney.com, July 10, 2007, http://money.cnn.com/2007/07/10/news/companies/newscorp/index.htm.

43. Ibid.

44. Paul R. La Monica, "Don't Bet on a 'Paper' Chase," CNNMoney.com, August 2, 2007.

45. Paul R. La Monica, "Getting Down to (Fox) Business," CNNMoney.com, October 15, 2007, http://mediabiz.blogs.cnnmoney.cnn.com/2007/10/15/getting-down-to-fox-business/.

46. Paul R. La Monica, "Now What, Rupert?" CNNMoney.com, August 7, 2007, http://mediabiz.blogs.cnnmoney.cnn.com/2007/08/07/now-what-rupert/.

Chapter 8: All in the Family

1. "Advice from Murdoch's Mom: Stay Busy," Associated Press, February 7, 2008.

2. http://www.newscorp.com/news/news_252.html.

3. Ibid.

4. http://phx.corporate-ir.net/phoenix.zhtml?c=104016&p=irol-newsArticle_Print&ID=143891&highlight=.

5. http://phx.corporate-ir.net/phoenix.zhtml?c=104016&p=irol-newsArticle_Print&ID=465898&highlight=.

6. Ibid.

7. Ibid.

8. McGraw-Hill Media Summit, New York, February 8, 2007.

9. http://www.newscorp.com/news/news_362.html.

10. http://www.newscorp.com/news/news_321.html.

11. http://www.newscorp.com/news/news_335.html.

12. House of Lords Select Committee on Communications testimony, January 23, 2008, http://www.publications.parliament.uk/pa/ld /lduncorr/comms230108ev15.pdf.

13. http://www.newscorp.com/news/news_214.html.

14. Ibid.

15. Paul R. La Monica, "Media to Tech: Stop Stealing!" CNNMoney.com, November 19, 2002, http://money.cnn.com/2002/11/19/technology /comdex_chernin/index.htm.

16. Ibid.

17. Citigroup Eighteenth Annual Entertainment, Media and Telecommunications Conference, Phoenix, Arizona, January 9, 2008.

18. Transcript of *Your World with Neil Cavuto*, Fox News, December 13, 2007.

19. Conversation with the author, March 6, 2008.

20. Citigroup Eighteenth Annual Entertainment, Media and Telecommunications Conference, Phoenix, Arizona, January 9, 2008.

21. Ibid.

Epilogue

1. House of Lords Select Committee on Communications testimony, January 23, 2008, http://www.publications.parliament.uk/pa/ld /lduncorr/comms230108ev15.pdf.

2. Bear Stearns Media Conference, Palm Beach, Florida, March 10, 2008.

3. http://www.newscorp.com/news/news_320.html.

4. *Judith Regan v. HarperCollins Publishers LLC,* 603758/2007, New York State Supreme Court (Manhattan).

5. http://www.newscorp.com/news/news_364.html.

6. McGraw-Hill Media Summit, New York, February 8, 2007.

7. Paul R. La Monica, "Private Equity May Buy the Book," CNNMoney .com, December 18, 2006, http://money.cnn.com/2006/12/18/news /companies/books/index.htm.

8. Ibid.

9. Paul R. La Monica, "Media Mergers: The party Is Over," CNNMoney .com, October 30, 2007, http://mediabiz.blogs.cnnmoney.cnn.com /2007/10/30/media-mergers-the-party-is-over/.

10. Personal notes from conference call, August 8, 2006.

11. Goldman Sachs' Communacopia XVI Conference, New York, September 18, 2007.

12. Conversation with the author, March 6, 2008.

13. Ibid.

14. Paul R. La Monica, "Sex Doesn't Sell," CNNMoney.com, September 20, 2006, http://money.cnn.com/2006/09/20/commentary/media biz/index.htm.

Additional Research Resources

Neil Chenoweth. *Virtual Murdoch: Reality Wars on the Information Highway.* London: Secker & Warburg, 2001.

Ketupa.net: A media industry resource. http://www.ketupa.net/index .htm.

Bruce Page. *The Murdoch Archipelago.* New York: Simon & Schuster, 2003.

Project for Excellence in Journalism: Publisher Murdoch's U.S. track record, http://www.journalism.org/node/6757.

INDEX

ABC, 4, 43, 46, 50–52, 54, 67, 73, 74,
    114, 145–46
Adelaide News, 14, 17, 194, 225
Adelphia, 211
Aiello, Paul, 121
Ailes, Roger, 64, 69, 73, 74, 76, 84–87,
    89–91, 200
Alterman, Eric, 103
American Idol, 5, 42, 56, 59
Annenberg, Walter, 118, 125
AOL, 116, 146
Apple, 115
AT&T, 134–36, 142
Atlanta Journal-Constitution, 73–74
Atorino, Edward, 174
Australian, 18

Ball, Tony, 207
Bancroft, Christopher, 183
Bancroft family, 2, 170–75, 178–87,
    189, 195
Bancroft, Natalie, 195–96

Bank, David, 94, 165
BBC, 87, 102, 103
Belo Corp., 38
Bennett, Robert, 137–38
Berlusconi, Silvio, 96–97
Bernanke, Ben, 88–89
Bertelsmann, 101
Bewkes, Jeffrey, 116, 217, 224
Big Ten Network, 72
Bilotti, Richard, 197–98
Black, Scott, 39, 198
Blair, Tony, 27, 96–98
Boehne, Richard, 38
Bonner, Joseph, 142–43
Booker, Patricia, 205
Boston Herald, 22, 34
Boyar, Mark, 179–80
Branson, Richard, 208
Breslow, Jordan, 200
Brin, Sergey, 155–56
Brown, Kevin, 123
Brown-Simpson, Nicole, 231–32

BSkyB, 87, 95–99, 105, 106, 118, 120–
    22, 128, 129, 132, 206–9, 213
Burkle, Ron, 2, 175, 183–84
Bush, George W., 86
BusinessWeek, 127, 196

Cablevision, 211
Campbell, Todd, 90
Capital Cities Communications Inc.,
    43, 46
Carroll, Bill, 238
CBS, 4, 50–52, 54, 55, 57–58, 67, 73,
    74, 93, 113–14, 217, 224
Chachas, John, 197
Chernin, Peter, 12, 60, 64, 116, 122,
    201, 214–25, 228
Chicago Sun-Times, 22, 33, 49–50, 117
Chicago Tribune, 169, 170
China, 33, 92, 101–11, 153, 188, 213–14,
    231
Chren, Michael, 184–85
Chris-Craft Industries, 56
Clinton, Bill, 68, 77
CNBC, 9–11, 64, 71, 85, 88–90, 175,
    176, 178, 179, 196, 197, 200
CNN, 5, 9, 67, 68, 70, 72–79, 84, 88–
    89
Comcast, 210–11
Consolidated Media Holdings,
    204–5
Courier-Life, 34
CW, 58–59

Daily Mail, 31–32
Daily Mirror, 18, 19
Dalai Lama, 104
Dauman, Philippe, 114, 217, 224

Davis, Marvin, 42, 45, 47–48
Deng, Wendi, 105, 107
Deng Rong, 102–3
Deng Xiaoping, 102–3
DeVoe, David, 60, 217
DeWolfe, Chris, 65, 152–53
Diller, Barry, 45, 48, 64–67, 85
DiMaggio, Joe, 232
DirecTV, 3, 63, 118, 128–30, 132–38,
    140–43, 227, 233, 236
DISH Network, 129
Disney, *see* Walt Disney
Dolan, Charles, 211
Dolan, James, 211
Dorfman, Richard, 18, 23, 66, 108–9,
    120–21, 221, 236–37
Dover, Bruce, 107–8
Dow Jones, 1–4, 7–10, 12–13, 15, 16, 33,
    34, 103, 104, 106–9, 127, 167,
    168–201, 221–22, 226–27, 230,
    236, 237

East and West (Patten), 104, 231
EchoStar Communications, 129–31,
    134–36, 211
Economist, 178
Eisner, Michael, 114, 216
Ellis, Eric, 107
Ergen, Charlie, 129, 131, 136
ESPN, 124, 145–46

Facebook, 7, 161–65
Falun Gong, 105, 213
Financial Times, 8, 119, 138, 171, 178,
    193, 195
FiOS TV, 135
Fonda, Jane, 81

Fortune, 12, 147, 153
Fox Broadcasting Company, 4–5, 11–
        12, 22, 42, 48–67, 73–74, 92,
        113, 117, 119–20, 153, 159, 189,
        214, 215, 229, 232, 237–38
Fox Business Network (FBN), 9–12,
        72, 84, 85, 88–92, 159, 176, 191,
        196–98, 200–201
Fox Entertainment Group, 61, 130
Fox Family Worldwide, 117
Fox Interactive Media (FIM), 62–63,
        147–67, 199
Fox International Channels, 91
Fox Kids Worldwide, 117
Fox News Channel, 5, 11–12, 64, 68–
        88, 90–92, 113, 132, 153, 189,
        194, 198, 213, 220
Fox Sports, 71, 204, 237
Frank, Betsy, 75
Free Press, 189
Freston, Tom, 114
Friedman, Jane, 231
FX, 71, 72, 84, 132, 237

Gemstar, 125–29
General Electric, 2, 9, 10, 69, 70, 83,
        93, 157, 175–80, 196–97, 217,
        229
General Motors, 129, 130
Giuliani, Donna Hanover, 81
Giuliani, Rudolph, 69, 79, 81, 232–33
Global Energy Initiative, 212–13
Goldman, Ron, 231–32
Google, 145–46, 154–62, 165, 166,
        177
Gore, Al, 86, 213
Gould, Alan, 2–3, 113, 127

Graham, Donald, 210, 211
Graham, Katharine, 210
Greenfield, Richard, 4
Greenspan, Brad, 175
Grimes, Larry, 176
Guthrie, Michelle, 121

Hanley, Rich, 188–90
Hannity & Colmes, 77
Harper & Row, 119, 231
HarperCollins, 41, 61, 102–4, 119–20,
        230–35, 237
Hartman, John K., 13, 35
Haverty, Larry, 13, 180
Heyward, Andrew, 75
Hill, Leslie, 183–84, 187
Hinton, Les, 194–95
Hodges, Craig, 38
Hoffman, Tony, 50
Hughes Corporation, 129–31
Hughes Electronics, 130–34
Hulu, 157, 158

IAPE, 173, 175, 182, 189–90
Icahn, Carl, 115–16
If I Did It (Simpson), 231–34
Iger, Robert, 114–15, 216, 219, 224
IGN Entertainment, 149–50
Illyria, 204–5
Independent, 82
India, 110–11, 121, 122
Intermix Media, 5–6, 148–49, 153,
        157, 159, 175
International Family Entertainment
        Inc., 117
Isgur, Lee, 44
ITV, 208

Jacobs, Bill, 135–36
Jamba!, 151
Joyce, David, 155, 183

Kerik, Bernard, 232–33
Kitman, Marvin, 85
Kosar, Bernie, 149
Kurtz, Howard, 76, 77

Lawrence, Glover, 234
Liberty Media, 3, 125, 128, 129, 137–43, 236
LinkedIn, 152
Los Angeles Dodgers, 3, 12, 123–24, 233

McCaffrey, Barry, 77
McChesney, Robert W., 189
McCourt, Frank, 124
McGlynn, James, 201
McGraw-Hill, 196–97
MacKenzie, Kelvin, 30–31
Malone, John, 3, 67, 82, 125, 128–29, 133, 137–43, 235–36
Manchester United, 97–98
Mantle, Mickey, 232
Mark, Morris, 116
Martin, Laura, 197, 199
Maxwell, Robert, 18
Mediaset, 96–97
Melbourne Herald, 17
Mendoza, Manuel, 76
Meron, Daniel, 117–18
Metrick, Andrew, 151
Metromedia, 45–48, 50, 52
Meyer, Eugene, 210

Microsoft, 2, 7, 160, 161–62, 165, 166, 177–78
Monroe, Marilyn, 232
Monster Worldwide, 152
Moonves, Leslie, 114, 217, 224
MSNBC, 74, 75, 78
Mukerjea, Peter, 121
Murdoch, Chloe, 17, 105, 206, 238
Murdoch, Elisabeth (daughter of Rupert), 205–6, 225
Murdoch, Elisabeth (mother of Rupert), 202
Murdoch, Grace, 17, 105, 206, 238
Murdoch, James, 105–6, 121–22, 203, 205–14, 221–25
Murdoch, Keith, 14, 16, 17, 225
Murdoch, Lachlan, 203–6, 215, 225
Murdoch, Prudence, 205, 206
My Father Deng Xiaoping (Deng Rong), 102–3
MyNetworkTV, 57–61
MySpace, 5–7, 59, 62, 65, 105, 106, 109, 113, 148, 151–66, 175, 199, 226

Nair, Sameer, 121
National Enquirer, 20, 21, 34
National Football League, 53–56
NBC, 4, 50–52, 67, 69–71, 73, 74, 83, 93, 157, 158, 176, 179, 217, 229
NDS, 117–18, 143–44
Neil, Andrew, 27–32, 214, 226–27
Newsday, 85, 169–70
News Limited, 17, 18, 20, 21, 31
News of the World, 7, 18, 19, 24–26, 30, 195

News Outdoor Group, 228
New World Communications, 55
New York Post, 6, 7, 21–25, 34, 47, 80–81, 169–71, 204, 213
New York Times, 11, 40, 44, 74, 86, 188, 189, 193
Nine Network, 44
Novosel, Dave, 230

O'Reilly, Bill, 6, 77
Owers, James, 190

Packer, James, 204, 205
Parsons, Richard, 116, 217
Patten, Chris, 103–4, 231
Pearlstine, Norman, 196–97
Pearson, 2, 8, 119, 171, 178–80, 196
Piazza, Mike, 123
Phillips, Reed, 37, 198–99, 234
Premiere AG, 100–101
Preston, Peter, 168–69
Prodi, Romano, 96–97

Rash, John, 58
Rattner, Steven, 8, 35–36
Redstone, Sumner, 113–14, 217
Regan, Judith, 231–34
Restall, Hugo, 107–8
Richardson, David, 143–44
Rigas, John, 211
Rigas, Timothy, 211
Riley, Emily, 152
Ritholtz, Barry, 89, 176
Roberts, Brian, 210–11
Roberts, Ralph, 210
Robertson, Pat, 117

Rosenberg, Howard, 76
Rupert's Adventures in China (Dover), 107–8
Russell, Bill, 123

Saban Corp., 117
San Antonio Express-News, 20, 34
Schiff, Dorothy, 21
Scout Media, 149
E. W. Scripps, 38–39
Shafer, Jack, 172
Shine Limited, 206
Simpson, O. J., 231–34
Simpsons, The, 5, 53, 215, 237–38
Sky Italia, 91, 94–96, 98–100, 118, 121, 122, 128, 129
Sky Network, 44
Sky News, 87
Sky Television, 95–96, 119, 120
Sorrell, Martin, 147
South China Morning Post, 119
Star, 20–21, 34
STAR TV, 91, 101–2, 103, 105, 106, 109, 121–22
Sterling, Greg, 161
Stream, 98–99
Suhler, John, 235
Sun, 7, 18–20, 23–27, 29–31, 171, 195
Sunday Times, 24–25, 27–29, 31, 195, 214

TCI, 82
Telecom Italia, 98–100
Telepiu, 99
Thatcher, Margaret, 24
Thomson, Robert, 195

Tibet, 104–5
Tierney, Brian, 2, 175
Time, 104, 182
Times, 24–25, 28–29, 35, 97, 195
Times Ledger, 34
Time Warner, 43, 58, 70, 79, 80, 82,
    83, 93, 112, 115–16, 142, 145,
    146, 160, 211, 217, 224, 234
Torv, Anna, 206
Triangle Publications, 118–20, 125
Turner, Ted, 5, 67, 68, 75–76, 78–83
Turner Broadcasting System, 79, 80
TV Guide, 3, 12, 119, 125–29, 233
20th Century Fox, 41–45, 47–50, 66

UPN, 57–58

Verizon, 134–36, 142
Viacom, 93, 112–14, 144, 146, 158, 160,
    217, 224
Village Voice, 3, 22, 33, 117
Virgin Media, 208
Vivendi Universal, 99, 101
Vogel, Harold, 51
VOX, 101

Wade, Rebekah, 19–20, 25–27, 29–32
Wall Street Journal, 1, 7–10, 25, 29, 37,
    76–77, 106, 108–9, 168, 170–
    71, 173, 175, 178, 180–83, 185–
    96, 198, 226–27, 237–38
Walt Disney, 13, 43, 44, 70, 93, 112,
    114–15, 117, 124, 144, 145–46,
    160, 216, 224, 228
Wang, Spencer, 200
Warner Communications, 43, 44
Washington Post, 46, 47, 76, 210
WB, 58
Weather Channel, 229, 230
Wright, Bob, 217

Yahoo, 146, 160–61, 165–66, 226
Yelland, David, 171
Yount, Steve, 189–90
YouTube, 157–58, 161
Yuen, Henry, 126–27

Zannino, Richard, 194
Zell, Sam, 169, 170
Zucker, Jeff, 217
Zuckerberg, Mark, 161